"This trim little book dissects the creation myth of America's premier National Park and in doing so raises important questions about the relationship between history and public memory."—*New Mexico Historical Review*

"This book is valuable because it offers a complex vision of the origins of the national park ideal rather than a simple campfire story, and it is accessible to general readers. It is also an interesting tale of the use, and possible misuse, of history."—Kathy S. Mason, *Register of the Kentucky Historical Society*

"The book should appeal to serious students of Western history and the conservation movement as well as those more philosophically inclined."—Mark Hertig, *Nebraska History*

"The discussion concerning the place of myths, legends, and solid history is thought provoking. For history graduate students it is a case study in how bureaucracy can change over a generation or two, how myths can begin, and how difficult it can be to destroy them."—Richard A. Bartlett, *Oregon Historical Quarterly*

"Well indexed and supported with numerous expanded reference notes."—Franklin J. Svoboda, *Natural Areas Journal*

"A short, crisp account. . . . By making the story more complex, more uncertain and more finely nuanced, Schullery and Whittlesey seek to make the tale 'more human—and therefore believable.' They seek not to break down the power of the myth through their careful inquiry, but rather to demonstrate its significance. . . . *Myth and History in the Creation of Yellowstone National Park* illustrates why the National Park creation myth resonates with the public and why National Parks provoke and express deeply held convictions."—*Montana Professor*

Myth *and* History
in the Creation *of*
Yellowstone
National Park

PAUL SCHULLERY
and
LEE WHITTLESEY

University of Nebraska Press
Lincoln and London

All author's royalties from this book will be donated to the Yellowstone Association, a nonprofit cooperating association that fosters education and research in Yellowstone National Park.

Library of Congress Cataloging-in-Publication Data
Schullery, Paul.
Myth and history in the creation of Yellowstone National Park / Paul Schullery and Lee Whittlesey.
p. cm.
Includes bibliographical references and index.
ISBN 0-8032-4305-7 (cl.: alk. paper)
ISBN 978-0-8032-3473-4 (pa.: alk. paper)
1. Yellowstone National Park—History. 2. Yellowstone National Park—Folklore. I. Whittlesey, Lee H., 1950– . II. Title.
F722.S375 2003
978.7'52—dc21
2003040994

To Robert Utley,
historian of the American West
and friend of the national parks

Contents

Illustrations

Acknowledgments

By way of disclaimer, we need to explain that we wrote this book while employees of the National Park Service in Yellowstone National Park. At many points we call into question interpretive practices of the agency through much of the twentieth century; we criticize, or expose flaws in, the thinking and decisions of several prominent figures in National Park Service history; and we expose what we believe was poorly considered, even unethical behavior by agency personnel. Despite these criticisms, at no time during our several years of researching and writing this book did we experience any pressure from National Park Service superiors or colleagues to moderate or in any other way alter our interpretations. It appears to us now that the most loyal remaining friends of the Madison campfire myth may be outside the agency.

Both of us have been conducting historical research on Yellowstone since the early 1970s, collaborating on analysis of early accounts for about a decade, and writing for publication on the ecological history of the greater Yellowstone region. In the process we returned frequently to the documentary record of the Washburn-Langford-Doane expedition, perhaps the most thorough observations of the Yellowstone region before the arrival of the first formal scientific surveys. Thus the issues there raised were repeatedly brought to our attention. After a while, we couldn't resist them any more.

Our work on this subject was first solidified into a presentation at "People and Place: The Human Experience in Greater Yellowstone," the fourth biennial conference on the Greater Yellowstone Ecosystem, held October 12–15, 1997, at Mammoth Hot Springs, Yellowstone National Park, Wyoming. We thank the conference organizers for their assistance and invitation. Our first publication relating to the Madison campfire story was based on the presentation given at this conference: Lee Whittlesey and Paul Schullery, "Yellowstone's Creation Myth," *George Wright Forum* 15, no.3 (1998): 80–87. We thank the editorial staff of the *Forum* for their interest in our investigation, which over the course of the next four years grew into the present book.

Of course, our work is also an extension of the research of the late Aubrey Haines, whose role in reconsidering the campfire story is documented here. Conversations and correspondence with Aubrey (beginning about twenty-five years ago) on the subject and the controversy over it have been most helpful. Since his death in 2000, his son Calvin Haines has generously assisted us in understanding the documentary trail that Aubrey left. And Yellowstone National Park administrative officer Joanne Timmins was of considerable help in sorting out issues relating to personnel actions that may have occurred during Aubrey Haines's career.

Over the years of our interest in this topic, communications with Robert Barbee, Richard Bartlett, John Good, Barry Mackintosh, Mary Meagher, Judith Meyer, Susan Rhoades Neel, Richard Russell, P. J. Ryan, Kim Allen Scott, Richard Sellars, and Robert Utley were likewise most useful. We also thank Lee Parsons for bringing the 1870 Yellowstone expedition journal of Henry Washburn to Yellowstone National Park for display in 1997.

The encouragement of director John Varley and deputy director Wayne Brewster, Yellowstone Center for Resources, and of Yellowstone superintendents Michael Finley and Suzanne Lewis is much appreciated. The staff of the Yellowstone National Park Research Library and museum collections provided their customarily outstanding help with locating rare documents and in other ways advancing our research. We especially thank Alissa Cherry, Katherine Lancaster Kirby, and Barb Zafft, librarians; Harold Housley, archival specialist; and John Dalheim, Beth Raz, and Sean Cahill, photo archives technicians. At the Montana State University Renne Library, Bozeman, special collections librarian Kim Allen Scott facilitated our work in many ways. At the Minnesota Historical Society, we appreciate the assistance of research supervisor Deborah L. Miller and the library staff and, at the Montana Historical Society Library, that of reference historian Brian Shovers, reference assistant Angela Murray, senior photo archivist Lory Morrow, and photo archivist Becca Kohl.

We are grateful to Lorraine Bonney, Wayne Brewster, Sue Consolo Murphy, Aubrey Haines, Barry Mackintosh, Dwight Pitcaithley, Marlene Merrill, Robert Utley, Michael Yochim and two anonymous reviewers for critical readings of various drafts of the manuscript. Finally, our thanks to the staff at the University of Nebraska Press for their interest in this somewhat unusual historical enterprise and for professional assistance in making the final book as good as it can be. We especially thank Patricia H. Sterling for her thoughtful and careful copyediting of the manuscript.

Introduction

According to popular tradition as presented in countless publications and public speeches during the past seventy-five years, the idea of Yellowstone National Park originated with one man on a specific day. As this tradition has come down to us, on the evening of September 19, 1870, members of the Washburn-Langford-Doane expedition (hereafter called the Washburn expedition or Washburn party) gathered around a campfire at the junction of the Gibbon and Firehole Rivers (called Madison Junction) in what would become Yellowstone National Park. They had just completed a tour of many of the area's most remarkable wonders, and, rather than lay claim to the region for personal gain, they had the idea of setting aside the geyser basins and surrounding country as a national park. The "campfire story," promoted and celebrated by several generations of conservation writers, historians, and National Park Service employees, became well established in the popular mind as the way not only Yellowstone but also national parks in general originated.

As early as the 1930s, however, historians doubted the tale or interpreted the park's creation differently. A variety of scholars have objected that the campfire story ignored known pre-1870 proposals that Yellowstone should be set aside for public use, that the process by which the national park was established did not seem to spring directly or indirectly from any such campfire conversation, and that the public-spirited sentiments attributed to the park's founders were not the only impulses driving their actions. In the 1960s and 1970s, Yellowstone historian Aubrey Haines and the academic historian Richard Bartlett cast further doubt on the story by suggesting, among other things, that even the campfire conversation itself was a historically dubious episode. Their revelations set off a round of debate and reconsideration in the National Park Service over the validity of the story and its usefulness to park staff as an educational device.

In both the National Park Service and the larger community of managers, scholars, and the public, the credibility of the campfire story has since gradually declined, though it is still often invoked by public speakers and in informal publications about Yellowstone. On August 17, 1997, during his speech at Mammoth Hot Springs as part of the park's 125th anniversary celebrations, Vice President Al Gore referred to the story and, though acknowledging that there was some debate over it, invoked its symbolic power.[1]

Similarly, in St. Louis, Missouri, on September 12, 2000, in a keynote address delivered to the entire national leadership of the National Park Service (more than a thousand top administrators and staff), Peter Raven, director of the Missouri Botanical Garden and one of the most honored and distinguished conservationists in the world (hailed by *Time* magazine in 1999 as one of its "Heroes of the Planet"), described the rapid expansion of the world's human population and the destruction of vital resources. He then said this: "Now [it was] against this background, this kind of disappearance of the frontier and lamenting values passed in the images of Eden that we're so comfortable with, that members of the Washburn-Langford-Doane Expedition gathered around their campfire near Madison Junction in Wyoming on September 19, 1870, and laid the plans that brought congressional action just eighteen months later to create Yellowstone as our first and one of our most wonderful national parks."[2] Whatever historians may tell us, then, there is no apparent lessening of enthusiasm for this story, especially on important ceremonial occasions. For all its flaws, many are still reluctant to let it go.

The persistence of the campfire story as a part of the culture of conservation should not be surprising. For one thing, though the story has been shown to be simplistic and not at all fair to the complexities of history, it has not and probably cannot be conclusively proved entirely untrue. For another, true or not, stories this deeply embedded in the thinking and self-perception of so many people do not yield to easy disregard. Their existence depends upon much more than mere provability. The campfire story has become a part of the historic and even the psychic fabric of the National Park Service and of the conservation community. And like any good story it reveals greater complexities the harder we look at it. Analysis of the campfire story demands that we ask a series of questions, some of which must remain unanswered until further information comes to light—which means that they may never be fully answered.

We consider these questions in more or less chronological sequence, beginning with the issue of who first proposed that the Yellowstone area be set aside as a public preserve or park. Next, we examine the documentary record left by members of the Washburn party themselves, not only their accounts of the campfire but also their published recollections of the entire expedition. We go on to observe the rise of the campfire story in the culture of the conservation movement, chronicle the various scholarly challenges to its specifics, and review the turmoil the National Park Service experienced as its most beloved institutional memory was reduced to folklore. We conclude with some observations on the vitality of the campfire story even today, when its diminished credibility still has not undermined its symbolic power.

*Myth and History in the Creation
of Yellowstone National Park*

CHAPTER ONE

In Camp That Night

More than twenty years ago, in his book *The Yellowstone Story*, Aubrey Haines reviewed the earliest known suggestions for a public park in the West, and specifically in the Yellowstone area. The story appears to have begun, at least remotely, with the artist George Catlin's suggestion, perhaps published as early as 1833 but certainly by 1843, that a significant portion of what is now western North America (from Mexico well into present Canada) be set aside as an immense "nation's park, containing man and beast, in all the wild freshness of their nature's beauty."[1] Though Catlin's suggestion made no reference to the Yellowstone region (then largely unknown to Euro-Americans) and had little or no known application to the later movement by which Yellowstone National Park was created (some of the founders may conceivably have read it, but none invoked it in their promotion), Haines was correct in citing it as indication of a sentiment, if only among a few people, in favor of preserving some wild lands from settlement.[2]

As Haines and other historians have noted, the rise of the park movement in Victorian America was expressed in such diverse institutions as Central Park in New York and the original Yosemite Grant of 1864.[3] There was without question a public consciousness of the worth of setting aside some lands, whether in wild form or in more cultivated and engineered ways, for public resort. In that climate it was probably to be expected that at least a few citizens would favor such an action to protect the Yellowstone region, though considering the generally exploitive mood of the United States in the decades following the Civil War, it would be foolish to expect such proposals to have automatically succeeded.

The first documented suggestions that Yellowstone be protected as a park or preserve occurred in 1865. As related by Father Francis Xavier

Kuppens, when a group of citizens of Montana Territory engaged in conversation at St. Peter's Mission with Kuppens and a Canadian man named Viell, who told of the wonders of the Yellowstone area, then acting Territorial Governor Thomas Meagher "said if things were as described the government ought to reserve the territory for a national park."[4] This account, though not published until 1897 and therefore perhaps suspect in its specifics (would Meagher have actually used the term "national park"?), is regarded as reliable proof of some discussion of the idea of setting aside the Yellowstone area for public enjoyment.

We see no reason to doubt the Kuppens account. The conversation apparently had numerous witnesses, and Kuppens does not seem to have had any particular motivation to generate such a tale falsely. His recollection is especially interesting because one of the people who apparently witnessed the conversation was Cornelius Hedges. Five years later, Hedges, according to his own account and that of Nathaniel Langford, was the member of the Washburn party to propose that Yellowstone be protected for the public. His presence when Meagher made his suggestion seems to cast a formidable shadow on later claims that Hedges originated the national park idea through personal inspiration alone. We have no way of knowing whether he was listening to Meagher, much less whether he remembered Meagher's remark five years later. But his presence in the room that day in 1865 when the remark was made must always weigh against the certainty that *his* national park idea was uninfluenced by the thoughts and ideas of others.

A second pre-1870 suggestion for the creation of Yellowstone National Park was claimed by David Folsom. In 1869, in the company of Charles Cook and William Peterson, Folsom visited the Yellowstone area on an exploring expedition that followed a route similar to that followed the next year by the Washburn party. Folsom later said that before leaving the area the three men agreed that it should be protected for public use.[5] According to the historian Hiram Chittenden, when Folsom and Cook wrote up their account for publication in the *Western Monthly*, the manuscript contained a "reference to the Park idea," but it was edited out before publication.[6]

In 1870 Folsom gave extensive advice to the Washburn expedition before it set out, and at that time, according to Folsom, he also imparted to Henry Washburn the idea of protecting Yellowstone. Folsom's possible role in advancing the idea becomes even more intriguing when we consider that in 1894, when Folsom's original account of the expedition was republished, Nathaniel Langford—of the Washburn party—provided a preface in which he made the following remarkable statement (emphasis added): "We trace the creation of the park from the Folsom-Cook expedition of 1869 to the Washburn expedition of 1870, and thence to the [Ferdinand] Hayden expedition (U.S. Geological Survey) of 1871. *Not to one of these expeditions more than to another* do we owe the legislation which set apart this 'pleasuring-ground for the benefit and enjoyment of the people.' "[7] This is more credit than Langford was willing to give Folsom, or Hayden for that matter, in his 1905 published account of the Washburn expedition (which we discuss later).

Folsom's recollection that he mentioned protecting Yellowstone to Washburn was corroborated by his 1869 traveling companion, Charles Cook. On July 14, 1922, during a celebration of the semicentennial of the founding of Yellowstone National Park held at Madison Junction, Cook spoke about their having camped "a little way up the Firehole River" from the junction in 1869:

> In camp that night we were talking over the great array of natural marvels we had seen and the scenic beauty of the area we had traversed.
>
> David Folsom, William Peterson and myself made up our party.
>
> Peterson remarked that probably it would not be long before settlers and prospectors began coming into the district and taking up the land around the canyons and the geysers, and that it would soon be all in private hands.
>
> I said that I thought the place was too big to be all taken up, but that anyway something ought to be done to keep the settlers out, so that everyone who wanted to, in future years, could travel through as freely and enjoy the region as we had.
>
> The[n] Folsom said: "The government ought not to allow anyone to locate here at all."
>
> "That's right," I said, "It ought to be kept for the public some way."
>
> Then we all expressed the same thought in different ways.
>
> None of us definitely suggested the idea of a national park. National parks were unknown then. But we knew that as soon as the wonderful character of the country was generally known outside, there would be plenty of people hurrying in to get possession, unless something was done.

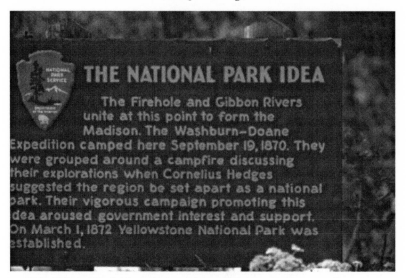

1. *"The National Park Idea." Sign at Madison Junction (August 1961). D. J. Brown, National Park Service photograph, Yellowstone Photograph Archives.*

We had this thought in mind when we came out a few days later and told others what we had seen.

Folsom made the definite statement to General Washburn that he hoped to see the Government step in and prevent private settlement. It was probably from this suggestion that the recommendation for the creation of the national park later arose in the minds of members of the Washburn-Langford expedition. And it was they who brought the proposal before Congress and got the national park act passed.[8]

The Folsom and Cook accounts have the same flavor as the Langford-Hedges story, to which we turn in the next chapter. That is, none of the three men (Folsom, Cook, Peterson) mentioned the conversation about protecting Yellowstone in their journals of the trip but only much later provided recollections of it. There is no particular reason to doubt that such a conversation could have occurred, however, beyond the persistent concern of historians that hindsight and selective memory tend to heighten rather than lessen the significance of a given event in the minds of the participants.

It is intriguing and somehow satisfying that both conversations were said to have occurred near the same location: the junction of the Firehole and Gibbon Rivers, now known as Madison Junction. On the one hand, members of both parties imply that at the time they assumed they had finished their exploration of the wonders of Yellowstone, even though they could not know what lay ahead as they traveled down the Madison River. Such an assumption smacks of an account written or modified with hindsight. On the other hand, if both conversations did indeed happen, there is a pleasant tidiness in their having occurred at the same place. Madison Junction, it seemed, inspired good talk.

There is no denying that the time was ripe for such conversations. As Haines has pointed out, it seems likely not only that ideas of preserving natural areas had become a part of the regional consciousness but also that Yellowstone itself had been considered as a possible candidate well before the Washburn party set out. The important questions raised by Haines, however, are whether the Washburn party members actually did talk about the idea of setting Yellowstone aside, and, if so, what effect the conversation had on the subsequent events that led to the creation of the park. What did the participants in the campfire conversation have to say about the night in question?

CHAPTER TWO

A Rather Unusual Discussion

The Washburn party left a surprising wealth of diaries, articles, reports, and letters describing the expedition's great adventure on the Yellowstone Plateau (see appendix). Regrettably few of these accounts dealt specifically with the party's activities on the evening of September 19. Not all members kept diaries, and some were not present that night, being involved in the search for the missing Truman Everts, who had become separated from the group near Yellowstone Lake.[1]

We begin with Nathaniel Langford, who, despite his not ever claiming to have originated the idea of establishing Yellowstone National Park, has long been the central character in this historical drama. Born in New York state in 1832, he had come west to mine gold in Idaho Territory in 1862. By 1864 he was prominent enough in territorial politics to be named collector of internal revenue for Montana Territory and in 1869 expected to be appointed (but, in the end, was not) territorial governor.[2] Among other distinctions was his involvement in famous episodes of vigilante justice in Montana between 1862 and 1866, about which he later published a minor western classic, *Vigilante Days and Ways* (1890).[3]

From 1872 to 1877, Langford served as Yellowstone National Park's first superintendent, while also holding full-time jobs elsewhere, including the post of U.S. bank examiner. Because his work in Yellowstone received no federal funding, a man with so many responsibilities, as Aubrey Haines observed, "could hardly be expected to do more than he did," which was visit the park three times during his superintendency and write one "annual" report.[4] His later life, after about 1876, was spent mostly in St. Paul, Minnesota, where he died in 1909.

Langford actually left two published accounts of the campfire conversation. The first appeared in his preface (cited in chapter 1) to Folsom's

2. Nathaniel P. Langford (circa 1889), member of the 1870 Washburn expedition to Yellowstone. Photographer unknown, National Park Service photograph, Yellowstone Photograph Archives (YELL 36590).

report of the 1869 Folsom-Cook-Peterson expedition to Yellowstone, which was published in 1894:

> Cornelius Hedges, of Helena, wrote the first articles ever published, urging the withdrawal of this region from private occupancy and dedicating it to the public, as a park. I distinctly recall the place and the occasion when he first broached the subject to the members of our party. It was in the first camp we made after leaving the Lower Geyser Basin. We were seated around the camp-fire, and one of our number suggested that a quarter section of land opposite the great falls of the Yellowstone would be a source of great profit to its owner. Another member of the party thought that the Upper Geyser Basin would furnish greater attraction for pleasure-seekers. Mr. Hedges then said that there ought to be no private ownership of any portion of that region, but that the whole of it ought to be set apart as a great national park. The suggestion met with quick and favorable response from all members of the party, and, to quote from a recent letter of Mr. Hedges to me, "the idea found favor with all, and from that time we never lost sight of it."[5]

But it was not on the basis of this brief recollection that the Madison campfire story developed into a historical institution. A far more influential account appeared in Nathaniel Langford's published "diary" (his word; like Haines, we prefer the term "reconstructed account"), which did not appear until 1905. A minor discrepancy occurs between the two accounts in that this more detailed version indicates one dissenting vote on Hedges's idea to create a national park. Though unnamed, the dissenter was almost certainly Jake Smith, whom Langford portrayed as a lazy ne'er-do-well.[6] Otherwise, the 1905 version is just a fuller and more animated rendition of the tale he outlined in 1894. Here is the full 1905 telling, from the September 20, 1870, entry in Langford's *Diary of the Washburn Expedition to the Yellowstone and Firehole Rivers in the Year 1870*:

> Last night, and also this morning in camp, the entire party had a rather unusual discussion. The proposition was made by some member that we utilize the result of our exploration by taking up quarter sections of land at the most prominent points of interest, and a general discussion followed. One member of our party suggested that if there could be secured by pre-emption a good title to two or three quarter sections of land opposite the lower fall of the Yellowstone and extending down the river along the cañon, they would eventually become a source of great profit to the owners. Another member of the party thought that it would be more desirable to take up a quarter section of land at the Upper Geyser Basin, for the reason that that locality could be more easily reached by tourists and pleasure seekers. A third suggestion was that each member of the party pre-empt a claim, and in order that no one should have an advantage over the others, the whole should be thrown into a common pool for the benefit of the entire party.
>
> Mr. Hedges then said that he did not approve of any of these plans—that there ought to be no private ownership of any portion of that region, but that the whole of it ought to be set apart as a great National Park, and that each one of us ought to make an effort to have this accomplished. His suggestion met with an instantaneous and favorable response from all—except one—of the members of our party, and each hour since the matter was first broached, our enthusiasm has increased. It has been the main

3. Lt. Gustavus Cheney Doane in dress uniform (1878). National Park Service photograph, Yellowstone Photograph Archives (YELL 7644).

theme of our conversation today as we journeyed. I lay awake half of last night thinking about it;—and if my wakefulness deprived my bed-fellow (Hedges) of any sleep, he has only himself and his disturbing National Park proposition to answer for it. Our purpose to create a park can only be accomplished by untiring work and concerted action in a warfare against the incredulity and unbelief of our National legislators when our proposal shall be presented for their approval. Nevertheless, I believe we can win the battle.

I do not know of any portion of our country where a national park can be established furnishing to visitors more wonderful attractions than here. These wonders are so different from anything we have ever seen—they are so various, so extensive—that the feeling in my mind from the moment they began to appear until we left them has been one of intense surprise and of incredulity. Every day spent in surveying them has revealed to me some new beauty, and now that I have left them, I begin to feel a skepticism which clothes them in a memory clouded by doubt.[7]

4. *Henry D. Washburn, leader of the 1870 expedition to Yellowstone (1869). Engraver unknown. National Park Service photograph of engraving, Yellowstone Photograph Archives (YELL 7684).*

"And right there," Yellowstone Superintendent Horace Albright would say fifty-two years later, "the national park idea was born."[8]

Setting aside for a moment the other "births" of the national park idea already discussed, contemporary corroboration for this particular version is impossible to come by. Only three of Langford's companion diarists seem to have commented at all on that evening's camp in the journals they kept during the trip. First, Lt. Gustavus C. Doane reported as follows at the conclusion of his entry for September 19:

> Following down the river bank through a deep canyon of volcanic rocks, in many places broken in huge fragments, we presently came to rapids, having a fall of perhaps 40 feet in half a mile. At this point the channel [of the Firehole River] narrows to 150 feet, and is shut in by perpendicular rocks. We were obliged to scale the ridge above, and follow down the stream on its summit, through dense timber and steep ravines, with considerable difficulty. In 3 miles we reached a level bottom, on the river, at the junction of a large creek [Gibbon River] coming in from the northeast. Camped at the junction. Distance, 18 miles.
>
> Barometer, 23.50; thermometer, 43°; elevation, 6,594 feet.[9]

5. Cornelius Hedges (n.d.). Photographer unknown, National Park Service photograph, Yellowstone Photograph Archives (YELL 7683).

Second, Henry Washburn, the party's admirable leader, also kept a diary of the expedition. Washburn, then surveyor general of Montana Territory, took ill (apparently he caught a cold) during the search for Truman Everts in the closing days of the party's exploration of the park area. He never fully recovered his health, and he died at the age of thirty-nine in Indiana in January 1871. His diary was known to exist in the early 1900s, and brief passages of it were quoted in print at that time, but then it was lost to public attention for many years. Thankfully, it has survived in the care of Washburn family descendants, who have granted historian Lee Parsons permission to work with it while preparing a biography of Henry Washburn. Mr. Parsons "debuted" the diary during the fourth biennial scientific conference on the Greater Yellowstone Ecosystem, in Yellowstone National Park, in 1997. Washburn's diary entries for the day of the supposed conversation and for the next day make no mention of the conversation.

Third, the man alleged to have proposed the Yellowstone National Park idea that evening was Cornelius Hedges. Born in New England in 1831, he arrived in Montana Territory in 1864 (having walked from Iowa). Though he did some mining, by 1865 he had opened a law office in Helena. Active in many community causes and organizations, he was named U.S. attorney for Montana in 1871, was a member of the Montana constitutional convention of 1884, and became a state senator in 1889. He died in Helena in 1907.[11] Hedges left the following conclusion of his entry for September 19 and beginning of his entry for September 20:

> made 20 miles today No fish in river. grub getting very thin. oposite a stream comes in on right side. mud bottom crossed another further back. shallow with gravelly bottom. said to be the Madison. Lieut says another came in on left soon after we started.

> Tues. 20. Didnt sleep well last night. got thinking of home & business. seems as if we were almost there. started out at 9 1/2 crossed river twice & travelled all day on right bank, about 8 miles along river.[12]

In 1904, when Hedges's diary was finally published in an edited version, he added the following passage as part of a larger footnote: "It was at the first camp after leaving the lower Geyser basin when all were speculating which point in the region we had been through, would become most notable that I first suggested the uniting all our efforts to get it made a National Park, little dreaming that such a thing were possible."[13] Although Langford had first put this basic story into print in 1894, Hedges's claim to patrimony of Yellowstone is based on this recollection from 1904, the first published mention he personally made of the campfire story.[14]

These, then, are the contemporary accounts of the camp of September 19, 1870, at the junction of the Firehole and Gibbon Rivers, and the later reminiscences of the conversation that reportedly occurred around the campfire that night, left by the only witnesses who chose to write about it—Nathaniel Langford and Cornelius Hedges. What stories did the campers tell of Yellowstone the next year after they got home?

CHAPTER THREE

On the Documentary Trail
from Madison Junction

If we had only their original reminiscences of the campfire conversation to work with, we would be hard pressed to evaluate the reliability of the published memories of Langford and Hedges. Fortunately, they and their colleagues left additional evidence—which has, however, caused considerable confusion among historians. Langford, especially, compromised his own story even as he took great pains to stand by it.

HEDGES'S HEROISM OR LANGFORD'S HINDSIGHT?

In 1894, in his preface to the Folsom account and at the same time that he was introducing the campfire story to the written record, Langford also made statements that would cause historians to wonder about the whole episode's historical legitimacy. As quoted in chapter 2, Langford put Hedges forward as the author of "the first articles ever published, urging the withdrawal of this region from private occupancy and dedicating it to the public, as a park." The specifics that Langford provided, however, undermined the very point he wished to make: "On our return, Mr. Hedges advocated the project in the public press. I have now in my possession a copy of the Helena *Herald* of Nov. 9, 1870, containing a letter of Mr Hedges, in which he advocated the scheme."[1] But here is what Hedges said in that letter (it was one letter, rather than the "articles" that Langford claimed) in the *Helena Herald*:

> This beautiful body of water [Yellowstone Lake] is situated in the
> extreme northwest corner of Wyoming, and, with its tributaries
> and sister lakes of smaller dimensions, is entirely cut off from all
> access from any portion of that Territory by the impassable and
> eternally snow-clad range of the Wind River Range of mountains.
> Hence the propriety that the Territorial lines be so readjusted that

Montana should embrace all that lake region west of the Wind River Range, a matter in which we hope our citizens will soon move to accomplish, as well as to secure, its future appropriation to the public use.[2]

Reading Hedges's remarks from the perspective of his own day, one is hard pressed to find in it any clear advocacy of a national park. In fact, it is mostly a plea for the reallocation of the public lands of the Yellowstone area, then in the Territory of Wyoming, to the Territory of Montana. Hedges apparently had great ambitions for his home territory, and he wanted to make it even bigger and grander than it was. His letter was, in other words, an attempt to grab land from a neighboring territory.

If we interpret as generously as we dare the letter's advocacy of "public use" of the area, the best we can come up with is that Hedges might have been in favor of some kind of territorial reserve, akin to a state park. But homesteading and sale of the land to private entities are also readily imaginable types of "public use," especially in light of the intense boosterism of the time. Difficulty of access to the Yellowstone Plateau by way of Wyoming Territory could have been what Hedges was referring to when he advocated the area's "future appropriation to public use." If the land belonged to Montana Territory, in other words, it would be easier to develop in any way. What did Hedges really mean?

Aubrey Haines interpreted Hedges's *Helena Herald* statements as follows:

A close examination of this suggestion shows it to have two distinct parts: one, calling for inclusion of what is essentially the present park within the Territory of Montana, and the other calling for a dedication to an undefined "public use." There is no way of divining what public use Cornelius Hedges had in mind, for he never elaborated on the idea. But subsequent statements in the Montana press indicate that a grant to the Territory of Montana, similar to the grant made to the State of California of the Yosemite Valley and Big Trees, was desired by some influential persons. Thus it is entirely possible that Hedges was thinking in the same terms.[3]

We agree with this assessment, adding only that yes, it was entirely possible, but Hedges's words give us no indication that he had already thought of that. In fact, it appears that the first statement from Hedges with a

6. Aubrey Haines at work in Yellowstone (March 1959). Photographer unknown, National Park Service photograph, Yellowstone Photograph Archives (YELL 43315).

clear recommendation of national park status for Yellowstone appeared in a memorial he wrote on behalf of the Montana Territorial Legislature to the United States Congress, urging Congress to consider that very reallocation. This occurred in early January 1872, some months after the "national park" term and idea had become conversational currency among journalists and park advocates (none of whom credited the idea to Hedges).[4]

A TANGLED TRAIL

It was in the process of unsorting this tangle of information, misinformation, and lack of information that Haines, during his tenure as park historian in the 1960s, became suspicious of Langford's 1905 account of the trip. Because of several irregularities there, Haines found himself in the uneasy position of questioning the fundamental creation story of the now venerable national park. The lack of mention of the conversation in the diaries of Washburn, Doane, and Hedges—especially that of Hedges—seemed to indicate that the party members did not see the conversation as such an important matter as Langford later made it out to be.

Other things increased Haines's uneasiness. Langford's own account in his published 1905 diary, the four-paragraph description quoted in the preceding chapter, could not be checked against his original "diary" because the original had disappeared. Haines discovered that of Langford's many diaries, the one dedicated to the 1870 Yellowstone trip was the only one missing from the Langford Collection at the Minnesota Historical Society (we confirmed its continued absence from this collection in 2001). Haines, who characterized Langford as a "literary string saver" (that is, an obsessive hoarder), wondered if the reason this one diary was missing had to do with possible later emendations made by Langford that altered the tone or content of the material dealing with the September 19 camp.[5]

Haines's suspicions about the campfire story were further reinforced by other Langford publications and public statements. For one, Langford's own contemporary writings—including a two-part *Scribner's* article (May and June 1871) and his manuscript of lectures given during the winter of 1870–71—make no mention of the campfire conversation or of the idea of creating a national park in Yellowstone.[6]

For another, there is the muddled episode of an alleged *New York Tribune* article that has puzzled historians for more than a century now. In the early 1890s, when Hiram Chittenden was preparing his own book *The Yellowstone National Park, Historical and Descriptive* (1895), Langford wrote him a letter supposedly quoting from a *Tribune* article of January 23, 1871, in which Langford spoke about turning Yellowstone into a national park. According to Langford, this passage, which Chittenden dutifully quoted, had appeared in the *Tribune* that day: "This is probably the most remarkable region of natural attractions in the world; and, while we already have our Niagara and Yosemite, this new field of wonders should be at once withdrawn from occupancy, and set apart as a public National Park for the enjoyment of the American people for all time."[7] But Haines found that no such article had been published in the *New York Tribune*. He also discovered that another potentially relevant item, Langford's clipping scrapbook covering that period, was—like his diary—missing from the Langford Collection at the Minnesota Historical Society. To Haines, as these coincidental gaps in the documentary record began to accumulate, Langford seemed to emerge as a slippery historical figure and a less than trustworthy reporter of his own activities.

Fortunately, a historian contemporary with Langford noted the same puzzling problems with Langford's report to Chittenden. In 1904, only a short time before Langford's reconstructed account of his Yellowstone trip appeared, Albert Matthews published an extended analysis of the word "park," much of which was about the establishment of Yellowstone National Park.[8] During his research, because he too was unable to find the *Tribune* article quoted by Chittenden, Matthews communicated directly with Langford to ask about the apparently nonexistent article. Here is the portion of Langford's response, by letter, which Matthews included in a footnote to his article:

> It is a matter of great surprise to me, that the quotation from my lecture referred to, cannot be found in the New York Tribune report of the lecture. I have in my scrapbook a report of the lecture, which I have always supposed was published in the New York Tribune of 23 January, 1871, and which contains the words quoted. The caption "New York Daily Tribune, Monday, January 23, 1871," was cut from the top of the Tribune, and is pasted in my scrap-book at the head of the report of my lecture. It seems almost incredible that I could have placed the Tribune caption over a report taken from another paper,—but if I made such a blunder, then what other paper was it? I cannot tell. Yet such a blunder might have been possible, considering the amount of matter which the various papers at that time contained in their eagerness to publish something concerning our discoveries, so marvellous and new to them.[9]

Matthews's sleuthing appears to have established that the missing Langford scrapbook did exist in the 1890s, for Matthews wrote to Chittenden about the affair and received this response: "I saw the clipping in question and copied it myself from Mr. Langford's scrap-book and on the border of it was noted, as is frequently done in such cases, the date and the paper from which it was taken."[10]

Where does this leave us in the question of Langford's reliability? Nowhere satisfying. Chittenden saw a clipping that said what he quoted it to say, but its true source and date cannot be established. As well, careful readers may notice that whereas Langford stated that he had clipped the actual name and date of the newspaper and pasted them in the scrapbook "at the head" of the article, Chittenden said that the name and date of the newspaper were "noted" on "the border," which we take to mean written out longhand in the margin of the clipping, as was and still is a common habit. This possible additional discrepancy would do

7. Hiram M. Chittenden, historian (circa 1910), who had early dealings with N. P. Langford on the campfire story and who erected an early memorial plaque at Madison Junction. Photographer unknown, National Park Service photograph, Yellowstone Photograph Archives (YELL 20358).

nothing for Langford's credibility, but we cannot be sure of Chittenden's meaning.

But Langford gave Matthews more on this subject (though it is unclear how many letters Matthews received from Langford, or how much of them he quoted), offering this recollection of his advocacy of the park (the ellipses and italics are as Matthews published them):

> Let us trace this matter from the beginning. While Mr. Hedges's proposition, made in the camp at the junction of the Fire-hole and Gibbon rivers, met with enthusiastic favorable response *at the time*, yet little more was thought of it by any of our party, except Hedges, for many months. . . . I do not think that my enthusiasm over the park project was roused to the working point until Hedges stirred me up. My lecture, as first prepared, was delivered both in Helena and Virginia City before I left Montana for the East, and contained no reference to the park project. After its delivery in these two places I modified it somewhat, interpolating many new paragraphs, of which the quotation in question is one: —and with all these changes the lecture was delivered in Washington and then in New York City. . . . Whatever reports of my

lecture have been made,—whether complete or incomplete,—the fact remains that I advocated the park scheme, in these few words, both in Washington and in New York City. Beyond a mere statement of this fact, in answer to interrogatories on the subject, I never claimed any credit for the advocacy. This belonged to Hedges.[11]

Matthews's correspondence adds some interesting dimensions to the issue and helps to settle some aspects of it. For example, we assume that Chittenden actually saw a real newspaper clipping in Langford's scrapbook. We assume as well that he copied it accurately. Assuming those things, we consider it certainly possible that Langford did in fact offer his advocacy statement during his New York and Washington speeches. Yet it seems odd that the surviving manuscript of the speech, in Langford's hand, does not contain such an advocacy statement. If he did revise the speech between Montana Territory and the East, the changes did not make their way into the only surviving copy.[12] Once more the coincidental gaps in the documentary record prevent us from checking Langford's statements, so that again, like Haines, we are left with an uneasy feeling about it all. It is clearly possible that Langford was being forthright in his communications with Matthews, but it is curious that the solid evidence to support his story is so consistently elusive.

Two other problems emerge from his letter. The first is that contrary to Langford's account of the Washburn party's enthusiasm for the park idea on September 19 and 20, according to this letter the participants all promptly forgot about it. Are these the hero-advocates who created Yellowstone, or not? Were they enthusiastic, or did they even care? The inconsistency between Langford's *Diary* account and the actual behavior of the expedition members is worrisome.

Perhaps as troubling is the almost breathtaking disingenuousness of Langford's closing statement, asserting that Hedges was the real hero— as if Langford's lifelong promotion of himself as one of the great pioneering figures of Yellowstone history did not occur. Deflecting certain elements of the glory to Hedges in no way proves that Langford did not intend to leave plenty for himself.

A SUSPICIOUS SILENCE

Another baffling question arises from an attempt to place the campfire conversation in the context of the entire Washburn party adventure: the matter of the party members' own notion of the importance of what they were doing. When these men set out from Fort Ellis, near Bozeman, for the Yellowstone area, they knew they were participating in an exploration of at least regional historical significance. Their trip was announced and celebrated in the regional press, and there was disappointment among others (including Philetus Norris, who would in 1877 become the park's second superintendent) who had hoped to go along. Many of the explorers were prominent citizens of Montana Territory, aware of their potential fame in that ambition-rich young political arena. In short, members of the Washburn party clearly had some sense of the enduring place that their discoveries would give them in the region's history.

Considering, then, all the trivial and less consequential subjects they found worth recording in their personal diaries, why do none of the others extant diaries make even the slightest mention of their momentous deliberations over the fate of the area—especially since, according to Langford, those deliberations not only consumed the evening of September 19 but also were "the main theme of our conversation" all day on the 20th?[13] The diaries of most were primarily confined to the basics of geography and unusual sites, but would not this singular conversation, which inspired such great enthusiasm, justify even a word or two?

Moreover, members of the Washburn party wrote much more than diaries. In fact, their eventual literary output recalls the famous characterization of Lewis and Clark as the "writingest" of explorers.[14] Their journals were only the first of their literary efforts about their adventure. By the following June, Washburn himself had published a two-part article in the *Helena Daily Herald*.[15] Trumbull published an article in the *Overland Monthly*, a two-part article in the *Rocky Mountain Weekly Gazette*, and a two-part article in the *Rocky Mountain Daily Gazette*.[16] Langford published a two-part article in *Scribner's Monthly*.[17] Hedges himself published five articles (in the form of long letters) in the *Helena Herald*.[18] Perhaps most important, Doane completed his formal report, which, by virtue of his role as military escort commander and federal government representative, was probably the closest thing the party had to an official history.[19]

This was a lot of publications.[20] And yet in none of them do members of the party make specific reference to the campfire conversation or, far more important, to any campaign for a national park or any sort of federal, state, or private reservation to protect Yellowstone. If indeed all but one of these men (as Langford maintained) agreed enthusiastically that they should "make an effort" to establish Yellowstone as a "National Park," why did none of them say so? These articles, read by thousands of people, would have been their best chance to promote so exciting a plan.

The failure of the entire Washburn party to speak out for the park idea is hardly the sort of ardent advocacy that Langford reported as existing among these men following their September 19 campfire conversation. And it is yet another reason for Aubrey Haines to feel justified in thinking that Langford's 1905 "diary" entry for September 20, 1870, supposedly recounting the events of the previous evening, rang hollow.

CHAPTER FOUR

Coming to Terms
with Nathaniel Langford

The gaps in the documentary record, the peculiarities and contradictions of Langford's own recollections, and the mysterious failure of Washburn party members either to mention the campfire conversation or to initiate a campaign for the creation of Yellowstone National Park all tend to make us as skeptical of Langford's campfire story as Haines was. But even without all these problems we would have trouble accepting Langford's story for the very simple reason that his first full telling of it, in his 1905 *Diary of the Washburn Expedition*, sounds phony.

As longtime readers of the journals and other writings of nineteenth-century western travelers, we have studied hundreds of firsthand accounts of journeys in and near the Yellowstone region. We have had reason to analyze these accounts closely in order to interpret them for possible ecological and other information. We do not claim that this experience has given us extraordinary skills in linguistics or content analysis, but it has undeniably allowed us to develop something of an ear for how people in those days expressed themselves in diaries and other informal writing. Perhaps it has also given us an eye for the emended account—the authentic contemporary report of an event that has undergone the editorial equivalent of cosmetic surgery to satisfy the needs of hindsight and embroidered memory.

To our experienced eyes and ears, Langford's account of the conversation around the campfire at Madison Junction on September 19, 1870, simply does not ring true. It has a contrived, manufactured thematic and structural tidiness that probably would not have characterized an authentic diary entry. His repeated use of the term "National Park" is suspect, partly because the term did not yet exist in common parlance and partly because no members of the party used it in anything they wrote over the course of the year following their expedition. Oddly, in

Langford's supposed diary, the term was sometimes capitalized, as if it were already a formal designation.[1]

As well, the paragraph in which Langford portrayed this group of men heroically girding their loins for the noble battle they somehow knew they would face has about it a strong sense of stage-setting. It sounds like contextual filler, placed in the narrative to suggest Langford's own savvy about political affairs: "Our purpose to create a park can only be accomplished by untiring work and concerted action in a warfare against the incredulity and unbelief of our National legislators when our proposal shall be presented for their approval. Nevertheless, I believe we can win the battle."[2] And yet Langford would have us believe that after such exhortation, after all this near-biblical bracing for battle, everybody just forgot about their "purpose" for a year. There is in this statement too much of confident presentiment. Like the rest of his account of the campfire conversation, it comes across as a little staged. It sounds too perfect.

The same reservations might be offered about much of the published Langford "diary." It has a polish, a depth, and a smoothness of narrative flow that would be very difficult to achieve in the hasty circumstances of a trip during which Langford's companions (except for Doane, who was expected to provide a detailed account) managed only fragmentary or even cryptic diary entries.

It is a great convenience to us that Langford's surviving statements anticipate our doubts. He claimed that his "diary" was published with few changes: "In reviewing my diary, preparatory to its publication, I have occasionally eliminated an expression that seemed to be too personal,— a sprinkling of pepper from the caster of my impatience,—and I have here and there added an explanatory annotation or illustration. With this exception I here present the original notes just as they were penned under the inspiration of the overwhelming wonders which everywhere revealed themselves to our astonished vision"[3]

Langford's position is clear and uncompromising. According to him, his is a real diary, virtually identical to the form in which he wrote it each night by the campfire. His assertion of authenticity challenges us, straight on, to believe him or not. Considering all the previously expressed problems with the campfire tale, and then adding our perception of the inauthentic tone of the published *Diary* of Nathaniel Langford, we must choose not.

Though historians and other observers are all too often blithely ready to call historical figures liars, such accusations should be made no more lightly than they would be made against living persons fully able to look us in the eye and defend themselves. And yet we simply do not believe Langford in this case. We do not know whether he was lying or made an honest mistake. We assume that he kept notes, perhaps very extensive ones, in his original diary, then transformed them for publication. What this means with respect to the authenticity of his account of the campfire conversation is impossible to say, but it seems highly unlikely that if a report of the campfire conversation appeared at all in the original journal, it could have been as long, as polished, or as forward-looking as the published version. Indeed, his extended direct quotations of people during the conversation would have been impossible unless his memory was exceptional or he took verbatim notes during the actual conversation, and we doubt either possibility.

In our examination of other surviving Langford diaries at the Minnesota Historical Society, we find that some of them are quite similar to the diaries kept by his companions on the Washburn expedition: that is, barely more than perfunctory notes. Still, that proves nothing about the missing Yellowstone diary. On such an important trip, Langford could well have written extensively because there was so much more to write about than on a routine business day. After all, his reports and other writings relating to his career, as well as his book on the Montana vigilantes, leave no doubt that he was readily capable of sustained literary production.

Allowing that Langford had the wherewithal to keep so detailed a diary, however, in no way proves that he did so. Because of the circumstances and problems just described, we still don't trust his claim that the 1905 publication was essentially a verbatim transcript of his original diary. In fact, it is our opinion that his claim to that effect sounds more like an attempt to deflect attention from the transparently altered and enlarged material in the published version. Among the occasions where we think that Langford might have played fast and loose with the facts, his claims about the authenticity of his published diary are in our opinion the most likely to be an outright lie—by which we mean not a casual error of fact but an intentional, premeditated falsehood intended to enhance his image.

At this stage in our deliberations, we find ourselves unavoidably detained by questions about the character of Nathaniel Langford. We reassert: it is no light matter to call a historical figure a liar, or even to accuse such a figure of wishful and well-intentioned distortion of the historical record. Having now done either or both of these things to Langford, we owe it to the man to look into his background, to see whether he was the kind of person to whom one should give the benefit of the doubt.

THE CHARACTER QUESTION

Aubrey Haines, with a thoroughness that was typical of his work, was not satisfied merely to dissect Langford's contribution to the literature and political development of Yellowstone National Park. Having encountered so much evidence of possible misbehavior in Langford's version of Yellowstone history, Haines devoted considerable time and energy to studying the rest of the man's career. None of the opinions he developed in this research appear in his published works, but he left a well-marked documentary trail in unpublished notes and letters, the sum of which is that Haines was not encouraged by his investigation. Langford seemed to him as questionable a character in the rest of his career in the West as he was in Yellowstone.

Haines had already concluded, for example, that Langford was "guilty of fraud in the matter of the purported *New York Tribune* clipping," but he admitted that he could not prove it and so chose not to make anything of it in his book. In examining the papers and other historical records surrounding Langford's career, however, Haines found more indications that the man was untrustworthy. His study of Langford's tenure as a collector of internal revenue for Montana suggested that Langford's activities ranged from the "petty subterfuge" of helping bilk a fellow revenue officer to the "morally reprehensible" attempt to take advantage of the collector's assigned percentage of collected moneys. In the latter case, Haines discovered a letter from Langford to a fellow conspirator in the attempt, Samuel Hauser, which Langford apparently knew was so incriminating that he instructed Hauser to burn it as soon as he had read it; for some reason Hauser did not, and the letter came to rest at the Montana Historical Society. Furthermore, Haines could find no evidence other than criminal—or at the very least unsavory—behavior to account for Langford's quick prosperity in Montana: "The fact that Langford and Hauser were able to establish a First National Bank almost immediately (both were poor men when they arrived in the Territory, and neither 'struck it rich' in the placers) hints that the scheme worked well enough."[4]

But no crime was ever demonstrated. Indeed, even if his actions were

8. *Samuel Hauser (circa 1875), member of the 1870 Washburn expedition to Yellowstone. Photographer unknown, National Park Service photograph, Yellowstone Photograph Archives (YELL 367).*

"morally reprehensible" on occasion, Langford seemed to be either legitimately free of criminal guilt or unusually gifted at avoiding actual prosecution. Neither Haines nor we could find a single case in which criminal charges were actually brought against him, much less a case in which he was convicted of a crime.

Considering some of the stormy moments in his career, this is saying quite a bit. On January 21, 1869, the *Helena Weekly Herald*, hot on the trail of some political intrigue, condemned Langford for what the editor perceived as party disloyalty. The actual issue at hand is not as important as the tone of the condemnation: "We do not deny that Mr. Langford deceived us, as he also deceived many others of the party. He was not the first man to barter away his honor for a mess of pottage, nor are we the only victims of misplaced confidence in the world."[5] In 1878, when a grand jury indicted the president of a Montana bank owned by Langford's friend Hauser, the indictment concluded that the "responsibility of the disaster to the said bank rests largely upon the shoulders of the United States Bank Examiner, as he was evidently guilty of gross neglect to those duties which the law especially directs him to perform in such cases."[6] The examiner in question at that time was Nathaniel Langford.

Our own research revealed other such condemnations and apparent close brushes with actionable misdeed, but it is always hard to make out just where Langford stood in the trouble.[7] He was a public figure, and he was intimately involved with taxes; in what age is such a person not likely—if not certain—to be reviled, either by resentful taxpayers or by political rivals? Indeed, historians have on some occasions singled out Langford for his strict and devoted interpretation of tax statutes.[8] Merely that he was accused or attacked in the press does not prove that he did wrong. That a grand jury faulted him for failure to perform his duties weighs more heavily. But again, the man was not prosecuted, much less proved guilty.

Our search for a clearer idea of the character of Nathaniel Langford was not especially successful. As a public figure he was almost certain to attract criticism, whether he was guilty of wrongdoing or not. In the contentious atmosphere of territorial politics it was relatively easy to get crosswise of at least a few newspaper editors. If Langford made substantial amounts of money in a suspiciously short time, or otherwise acted in ways we now find troublesome, he seems to have managed so perfectly that prosecution was impossible. If he was guilty of political intrigues and partisan politics, he was merely typical of many American citizens of his time and place. After all our investigations, the worst that we might say about Langford is that though there is not enough evidence to suggest a regular pattern of questionable behavior, there was something unsavory about the way that he always seemed, no matter where he was or what his actual duties might have been, to be standing right next to the till.

Yet against these unconsummated accusations, vague suspicions, and outright rumors there stands a formidable body of positive testimonials that would warm the heart of any historical figure. Nathaniel Langford was widely memorialized as an honored citizen, even during his lifetime. Beginning as early as 1885, when he was profiled in *History of Montana 1739–1885*, the distinctions of his career as a pioneer financier, as a participant in the Vigilance Committee, as the first superintendent of Yellowstone National Park, and as a leading figure in the Masonic Lodge have all been repeatedly brought to print.[9]

Of course, the standard biographical dictionaries published in various states and regions a hundred years ago had little room for criticism; they were as boosterish as the men they celebrated. Even so, it was some indication of a citizen's reputation to be profiled in such works. Henry Castle, in *History of St. Paul and Vicinity* (1912), writing only the year after Langford's death, said that "the man was best known by a few intimate associates. Whatever praise the public has given the official these intimates have taken as a matter of course, for the able and fearless official is made of rugged manhood, sharpened by intelligence and tempered in strength of character."[10] The anonymous author of *Minnesota and Its People* (1924) concluded a glowing account of Langford's long life by stating that he "was widely known and universally honored and his labors were an effective element in promoting the civilization, improvement and progress of the west."[11] Little more, in the lights and moods of the time, could be asked of mortal man than that. His two-column entry in the redoubtable *Dictionary of American Biography* never rises to such rhetorical heights, but neither does it slip from the obvious conviction that Langford was a fine, upstanding, hardworking citizen of distinction.[12]

Again, the skeptic can glibly point out that many a politician who, millions were convinced, was an utter scoundrel has been widely and generously lionized upon his death. But the issue is not whether these praises were perfectly accurate; they certainly weren't (they typically overstated his role as Yellowstone superintendent, for one thing—as Langford himself tended to do). The greater issue here is that whatever he did right or wrong, he made it into those relatively rarified ranks of the leading citizens of his region and his generation. If we choose to take this historical reality cynically, we might say that whatever he did wrong, he got away with. If on the other hand we take it at its most affirmative, we might say that if he indeed was criticized and attacked by his opponents, he seems not to have lost his way under the burden of their disapproval. However we choose to judge Nathaniel Langford—as a slippery opportunist, a well-intentioned do-gooder with a poor memory for details, or in some other way—we had best begin by accepting that he passed from this world with his honor as intact and respected as any prominent citizen of his age might wish.

WHAT CAN WE KNOW ABOUT THE CAMPFIRE CONVERSATION?

The evidence that the campfire conversation did not occur is all negative. That is, we may lack convincing evidence that it happened as Langford claimed, but we have no proof that it did *not* happen. For support of its existence we are entirely dependent on the reminiscences–twenty-four years later—of two people, Hedges and Langford, one of whom stood to gain great glory for originating such an important idea as the national park; the other, to bask in the considerable reflection of that glory. But though Langford is a suspicious character in this context, we find no reason to suspect that Hedges is. Like Haines, we find Hedges to have been an honorable man whose motivations were as honest as they were straightforward.

Several members of the Washburn party were still alive when Hedges's journal (1904) and Langford's book (1905) were published.[13] In Langford's defense, therefore, we must say that it seems improbable for him to have fabricated the whole campfire conversation story on the assumption that none of his expedition companions would see the book and challenge it on that point.

It seems most likely to us, then, that there was at least some kind of conversation—if brief or less compelling to the participants than Langford claimed—dealing with the question of the fate of the wonders of Yellowstone. It also seems probable that Langford, from the longer perspective of thirty-five years later, embellished not only his diary entry but also the event itself, turning what might have been a minor conversational topic among many other topics into something far more detailed and momentous.

That said, there is more to learn about Langford and what might have been on his mind that night by the campfire.

CHAPTER FIVE

Altruists and Realists

There is more that attracts us to the campfire story than its questionable account of the rise of the idea of national parks. What made the story so special to generations of park enthusiasts, and such a wonderful device for park promoters and defenders, was that it presented the founders as motivated solely by a spirit of unselfish good will.

> The story portrayed the park idea as having such intuitive force of rightness that it was immediately embraced by all who heard it. For park managers seeking to justify or enlarge their meager budgets, the campfire story provided a rhetorical position of moral unassailability. It also provided the park movement with perfect heroes: altruists who were so committed to protecting wonder and beauty that they would forgo all thought of personal gain. And it put the creation of the park movement in the hands of the people whose possession of it would have the most symbolic power: regular citizens.[1]

Haines's earlier investigation into the campfire story, though, especially into the character and behavior of Nathaniel Langford, casts a shadow on the traditional view of the Washburn party as altruists, purely motivated by good will toward society. To understand the campfire story and to do justice to its role in history, one must know more about the motives and ambitions of the men who were there that night.

Haines, predictably, led the way in this question too. He discovered that before the 1870 expedition set out, Langford had visited financier Jay Cooke in Philadelphia. As an enthusiastic Montana booster, Langford had been interested in developing regional commercial transportation at least since December 1864, when the territorial legislature gave him and some associates a charter for a stage line from Virginia City to Emigrant

Gulch, on the Yellowstone River near present Emigrant, Montana.[2] At the time of their meeting, Cooke was seeking financing for the Northern Pacific Railroad. Though Langford's diary for that time does not reveal what specific topics were covered during their extended conversations on June 4 and 5, 1870, Haines thought it very likely that the two discussed possible advantages that might accrue to Cooke's railroad if the Yellowstone region turned out to be as extraordinary a place as earlier travelers had reported.[3] Whether they did or not, it was at this time that Langford officially joined the "corps of lecturers" funded by Cooke "to expedite the sale of Northern Pacific Railway bonds by popularizing the region through which the line was to be built."[4]

Here the glow of altruism is tarnished by the corrosion of commerce. Langford may not have thought of the national park idea yet, but long before September 19 he must already have been thinking hard about the commercial possibilities of the region and looking for good selling points. His later behavior on the 1870–71 winter lecture tour (funded by Cooke's railroad) proved he had found the best one of all: his lectures dealt not with the economic possibilities of Montana Territory but with the wonders of Yellowstone.[5]

Of course, similar and equally unrestrained sentiments in the promotion of Yellowstone and therefore Montana were expressed by Hedges in his resolution, sent by the Montana Territorial Legislature to the United States Congress, which proposed that Wyoming divest itself of the entire Yellowstone region, leaving it to the proprietorship and considerable advantage of Montana. These were men of their time, when boosterism was regarded as good citizenship. With no pangs of conscience, a man could do well personally while doing good publicly.

The desire for personal gain, or economic advancement of one's region and therefore oneself, does not prove that Langford or Hedges were doing something sinister. But it does cast a dramatically different and far richer light on what may have happened around the campfire on September 19. Of all the members of the Washburn party, only Langford, Hedges, and to some extent Hauser seemed later to take a visibly active role in promoting any protection for Yellowstone. And only Langford, funded by the Northern Pacific Railroad on his speaking tour in the winter of 1870–71, seems to have invested much time in it. Moreover, it seems certain to us that by September 19, Langford's hopes for Yellowstone as a railroad traffic generator must have been higher than ever. The expedition had found Yellowstone all it was rumored to be, and more. There were wonders galore, and the men of the Washburn party, as Langford himself noted in his reconstructed account, were already thinking of ways to cash in on them as they settled around the fire that evening. It was obvious that someone was going to make a lot of money here someday.

But if Langford was anywhere near as smart as we think he was, he could easily see the bigger picture and take the longer view of this opportunity: the greatest moneymaking resource of Yellowstone was the tourist, and that resource, properly developed and managed, could pay handsomely forever. Even had Langford not been an agent of the Northern Pacific Railroad that night, he might well have seen that the Yellowstone that would pay himself and his territory most handsomely was not a partitioned-off selection of independent tourist attractions but a larger, even public, reserve of some sort. Whether Hedges made his famous suggestion or not, and whether the rest of the group embraced it or not, Langford could have been expected to have some sympathy with the national park idea.

It is easy and perhaps helpful in this context to add an even more conspiratorial, almost comic, cast to the campfire conversation. To put the darkest possible complexion on the events of that evening, imagine Langford by the fire, happily daydreaming about how well this was all working out for his employer. Picture him mentally composing his letter to Jay Cooke and thinking about the stirring speeches he would give when he went back east in the coming winter to stump for the Northern Pacific.

Then, through his optimistic haze, he picks up the thread of the conversation around him and thinks something like this: "What's this? The boys are talking about divvying up the place! Staking claims to the geysers and falls! This will never do! Mr. Cooke will have a cow! But wait, what's Cornelius babbling about? Why, bless his heart, he's taking them on the high road—public good, the common people, future generations, and all that. And look, they're buying it (well, all of them except that reprobate Smith, of course). Whew! That was close, but this is going to work out fine; I couldn't have done much better myself!" As he hears the others fall into line in support of this vague but preferable Yellowstone future, Langford relaxes and returns to his earlier reverie: "Hmm. Some kind of public reservation. Might not be a bad idea at that. Mr. Cooke will be pleased."

Of course, this little scenario is purely manufactured—far more so than we think Langford's own version was—but it is not without its grain of painful truth. There is reason to take such a baldly conspiratorial view of Langford's promotion of the idea of Yellowstone as a federal reservation. Public ownership of the region's resources would certainly serve the railroad's interests better than an unruly patchwork of private holdings, and federal control would be much simpler to manipulate than private control. In one of the most damning accusations he would level, Aubrey Haines suggested that the reason Langford was such a lackadaisical and unproductive first superintendent of Yellowstone (1872–77) was that his real goal was to keep the park free from unwanted commercial development and competition until the railroad could get its tracks into the area and develop its own businesses there.[6]

We share Haines's suspicion of Langford's conduct as superintendent. Here again, as with his publications, Langford had a wonderful opportunity to further the cause of the park and ensure its enjoyment by the public. Even though his job was made difficult by a complete lack of funding, had he really wanted to advance the cause of public enjoyment of Yellowstone, he could have done so through the establishment of visitor services, simply by granting concessions to qualified applicants. But Langford seems to us to have used his concession-granting authority not to get the park rolling as a viable visitor attraction but to keep it as business-free as possible. During his five-year administration he routinely denied applications for concession permits, obstructing rather than advancing visitor services.[7] In Haines's view, and in ours, this looked more like serving the railroad interests than serving the public.

At this point in the analysis of the campfire story, it may seem to have reached such a low point of skepticism and cynicism that there is no recovery. The Washburn party did not originate the national park idea. The party's members did not rise from their blankets on September 20 and rush off to tell the world about their great dream of a national park. And the only one of them to put a lot of personal energy into the campaign for the creation of Yellowstone National Park was on the payroll of the one private corporation that stood to gain most from the creation of the park. Then, once the park opened, he effectively restricted visitor services throughout his five-year administration.

Admittedly, this is not as pretty a picture as that represented by the old campfire story. It is in fact a very complicated picture. There was altruism, but there was also apathy and maybe even avarice. The story that generations of park lovers came to count on for inspiration is gutted. What is left here to believe in?

Rest assured that there is much to believe in. Before considering the long life of this apparently indestructible story, we must pause long enough to celebrate the gains that come from abandoning it. Our careful and certainly painful inquiry into a beloved tradition leaves a far more human—and therefore believable—tale in which real people accomplished real good, however complicated their reasons. Letting go of the shallow legend permits a continuing inquiry into the wealth of subtlety, complexity, and wonder that characterizes any fully examined human institution. As delightful as the idealized old campfire story was, it hardly did justice to the richness and satisfactions of what really happened. After all, whatever led to it, and whoever was responsible, Yellowstone National Park was created, and it thrives even yet.

Besides, before we get too proud of our devotion to historical integrity and higher truths, it is good to keep in mind that we have, after all, only replaced one tale with another and that the new one is not likely to serve us forever, either.

CHAPTER SIX

Spreading the Word

The process by which the campfire story became institutionalized in the annals and consciousness of the National Park Service was a simple one. It was published, it was believed, and it was loved. For the first half-century or so after its publication in Langford's 1905 *Diary*, it seems to have been almost universally accepted as the complete story.

And why not? It came from Langford and Hedges, already long ensconced in the pantheon of Yellowstone's original pioneer heroes, and it was just the kind of story a great institution like Yellowstone deserved, or seemed to require. Why resist such perfection? As one former Yellowstone superintendent, Lemuel (Lon) Garrison, would write in 1971, when the story was under attack and reconsideration by several historians, "If it didn't happen we would have been well advised to invent it. It is a perfect image. Let's use it!"[1]

It was put to use almost immediately after its publication in Langford's 1905 *Diary*. The F. J. Haynes Company, the park concessioner that had published Langford's book (thus providing a powerful commercial lift for the tale), told or referred to the campfire story in successive editions of its extremely popular *Haynes Guide* from 1906 on. The first version read: "At the junction of the Gibbon and Firehole Rivers, the source of the Madison River, is National Park Mountain, historical from the fact that while the Washburn exploring party was camped there on Sept. 19, 1870, it was suggested by a member of the party (Mr. Cornelius Hedges) that this section should be set aside as a National Park, and it was through the efforts of the party and others that Congress in 1872 set aside this region as YELLOWSTONE NATIONAL PARK."[2] (The date of origin of the name of "National Park Mountain" is uncertain; in the period between 1906 and 1910, "Yellowstone Mountain" was also occasionally used, but National Park Mountain was the name that stuck.)

The campfire story was occasionally adjusted. In the 1908 *Guide*, the "others" whose efforts had been vaguely acknowledged in 1906 were deleted, so that it was solely through the efforts of the Washburn party "that Congress in 1872 passed the act of dedication."[3] In the 1912 edition some slight equivocation was restored: "It was largely through their efforts that Congress in 1872 passed the act of dedication."[4] Whether these changes were made because Haynes had learned more or were simply minor editorial adjustments with no particular motivation, we do not know. The phrasing did not change again for several years, until the entry for National Park Mountain was shortened and credit for efforts to create the park were removed entirely from the discussion for a time, replaced in the 1919 edition with a recommendation to see Langford's book for more details.[5]

Apparently some time in the ten years following the communication between Langford and Chittenden (chapter 3), Chittenden decided to celebrate the Washburn party and, according to Langford, ordered a "large slab" placed at Madison Junction bearing a sign:

JUNCTION
OF THE
Gibbon and Firehole Rivers,
Forming the Madison Fork of the Missouri.
ON THE POINT OF LAND BETWEEN THE TRIBUTARY STREAMS,
SEPTEMBER 19, 1870, THE CELEBRATED WASHBURN EXPEDI-
TION, WHICH FIRST MADE KNOWN TO THE WORLD THE WON-
DERS OF THE YELLOWSTONE, WAS ENCAMPED, AND HERE WAS
FIRST SUGGESTED THE IDEA OF SETTING APART THIS REGION
AS A NATIONAL PARK.[6]

We have not been able to determine what became of Chittenden's original "slab" sign. In the 1916 *Haynes Guide* there appeared a photograph of a wooden sign then in place at Madison Junction. It read: "Junction of the Gibbon and Firehole Rivers / Forming the Madison Fork of the Missouri / On the Point of Land Between the Two Tributary Streams / September 19th 1870 the Washburn Expedition Which / First Made Known to the World the Wonders of the Yellowstone / Was Encamped and Here Was First Suggested the Idea / Of Setting Apart This Region as A National Park.[7]

It was probably enough that the campfire story had behind it the full weight and prestige of the Haynes name, and the remarkable credibil-

9. *Interpretive sign at Madison Junction (circa 1910). H. B. Weatherwax scrapbook, Yellowstone Photograph Archives (YELL 129778).*

ity and circulation of the *Haynes Guide*. Decade after decade, each new edition was perhaps the foremost informational voice of Yellowstone. These little books had a nearly scriptural authority in the eyes of the park's devoted friends, and we both remember, in our early years of working there, how often older visitors and staff would lament the final demise of the series when the Haynes family left the park. At the very end of the *Guide*'s long, prosperous run, in the final (1966) edition, the campfire story was essentially unchanged from 1906:

Just beyond the junction of the Firehole and Gibbon Rivers,

10. Stephen T. Mather (n.d.), first director of the National Park Service. National Park Service photograph, Yellowstone Photograph Archives (YELL 125506–1).

which form the Madison River, is National Park Mountain (7,560 ft.) named to commemorate the discussion which led to the founding of Yellowstone National Park and the development of the National Park System. The discussion took place Sept. 19, 1870 in the camp of the Expedition of 1870 near the foot of this mountain opposite the junction of the streams. Cornelius Hedges is credited with having first made the suggestion that the region including the awe-inspiring, curious manifestations of nature, which that expedition had just visited should be made a national park.[8]

As an early promoter of the campfire story, Haynes soon had enthusiastic help. The leadership of the new National Park Service (established 1916) was quick to recognize the story's rhetorical force and excellent potential for publicity. Stephen Mather, the first director, and Horace Albright, Yellowstone superintendent from 1919 to 1929 and director of the National Park Service from 1929 to 1933, were—like Haynes—skilled publicists. They were always seeking ways to promote the high ideals and increased public use of the national parks. In the agency's first annual report—a milestone document in park history for its thoroughness and value as an educational tool among lawmakers unfamiliar with

11. Horace Albright (left), Charles Cook, and Ann Anzer at Madison Junction, fiftieth anniversary celebration (1922). Photographer unknown, National Park Service photograph, Yellowstone Photograph Archives (YELL 106393).

the parks and their needs—the origin of the park idea was given early prominence:

BIRTH OF THE NATIONAL-PARK IDEA

The first national park to be set apart was the area embracing the hot springs of Arkansas. The reservation of this land was made April 20, 1832. However, it was nearly 50 years after the act of reservation before steps were taken to develop the park in the public interest. In the meantime the remarkable area which is now Yellowstone Park had been discovered and explored, and the famous Washburn-Langford party in its camp near the junction of the Firehole and Gibbon Rivers [here the report cites the 1915 edition of Chittenden's history and Langford's book] in the Yellowstone region had conceived of the "national park" idea [here

12. The 1869 explorer Charles Cook (center), Park Superintendent Horace Albright (right), and W. A. Hedges, descendant of Cornelius Hedges, pose together near Madison Junction at fiftieth anniversary celebration of Yellowstone National Park (1922). National Park Service photograph, Yellowstone Photograph Archives (YELL 37153).

citing Chittenden and Langford again], [had] placed a broad unselfish, public-spirited construction upon the term, and had brought the wonders of the region and the splendid patriotic national park plan to the attention of Congress, with the result that, on March 1, 1872 [here citing the relevant U.S. statutes], Yellowstone National Park was established.[9]

Speaking of the "rare foresight of the pioneers," Mather referred both to the Washburn party and to the legislators who acted to save the park.[10] By the time of the Yellowstone semicentennial celebration of 1922, there was no question that the Madison campfire story was the cornerstone of any exercise honoring the creation of the park.

It may, however, surprise historians familiar with the aggressively promotional stance taken by Mather and Albright to learn that as park superintendent, Albright was reluctant to take on the additional duties associated with celebrating this important anniversary. Despite receiving numerous enthusiastic letters from concessioners and the travel indus-

13. Woodcut drawing of Washburn-Langford-Doane campfire by W. S. Chapman. From Merrill D. Beal, The Story of Man in Yellowstone *(Caldwell ID: Caxton, 1949), 143. Courtesy Bill Chapman.*

try about the great advertising opportunities provided by an anniversary celebration, Albright repeatedly stated that he lacked time and staff to pull off such an event.

In May, Mather wrote to Albright, suggesting that because of the burden of routine business with increased travel to the park, "we don't want to attempt too much. Furthermore, if you were to have a pageant at Mammoth [Hot Springs], the even distribution of visitors over the park would be unsettled, not only for one day but for several, and it would probably result in a congestion that might be disastrous and give us a black eye. All in all, I think the thing to do is to celebrate the semicentennial quietly throughout the season." Concluding that he would consider something more ambitious if the "railroads and the park operators would agree to bear all expenses and to make arrangements under your general approval," Mather left it to Albright to work out the best approach.[11]

These deliberations were occurring just weeks before the season opened (by contrast, planning for Yellowstone's 125th anniversary in

1997 began two years in advance, though staff overload was accurately foreseen even then), and Albright soon settled on a celebration of one day, July 14, at Madison Junction. It was here that an aged Charles Cook told the story of the 1869 conversation he had with Folsom about setting Yellowstone aside. Albright himself retold the Langford version of the Madison campfire. As part of the celebration, Cornelius Hedges's sons planted a tree "to mark the spot where their father stood when he proposed making this unequaled region a national park."[12]

With this firm a foundation, it is no wonder that the campfire story flourished. Countless ranger-naturalist programs throughout the national parks featured the story, as did books and articles without end. Even into the late 1960s and early 1970s, heroism was probably the most widely acclaimed quality associated with members of the Washburn party, and a significant part of that acclaim resulted from their recognized role in the creation of Yellowstone National Park.

CHAPTER SEVEN

The Debate

For the purposes of this book, we would prefer to concentrate on the process by which the story was questioned rather than on its universal spread from modest park publications to such public forums as a 1963 performance of the campfire conversation on the *Hallmark Hall of Fame*.[1] It may be enough to say that between 1920 and 1970 the American public probably received more exposure to the creation story of the national parks than to that of any other federal agency.

Yet there seems always to have been some concern over the credibility of the story. In the 1927 *Ranger Naturalists Manual of Yellowstone National Park*, for example, the tale is told repeatedly by the manual's multiple authors, but Ranger Robert H. Dolliver seemed to have done some reading or listening that caused him to complicate it slightly. After repeating the usual version of the conversation, with Hedges standing up and proposing the preservation of Yellowstone, Dolliver elaborated: "Although Mr. Hedges deserves the credit for suggesting the right thing in the right place first, many other men, some of them before Mr. Hedges and certainly many afterwards, had this same idea and worked hard for it."[2]

By 1932, when Louis C. Cramton published his important monograph *Early History of Yellowstone National Park and Its Relation to National Park Policies*, there was considerable need for cleaning up the story of the park's origin, even aside from the campfire story's growing popularity. A number of names had been put forth as having led the campaign to create the park, some important and others entirely without merit. Cramton devoted several pages to sorting out this list of Yellowstone paternity claimants. He noted that the story of the campfire conversation as published in Langford's 1905 *Diary* was supported by no other contemporary account, and also noted that the *New York Tribune* article

14. Louis C. Cramton, historian and congressman (1932), at Lake Mead National Recreation Area. National Park Service photograph, Harpers Ferry Center.

cited by Chittenden did not exist, but he did not openly challenge Langford's story. Instead, he concluded that Folsom, Hedges, Langford, and Hayden, along with several senators and congressmen, had all played important roles.[3]

By demonstrating that credit for the creation of the park was in fact diffuse and widespread, Cramton may have inadvertently helped establish a mood contrary to the simplistic campfire story. Certainly he led

15. Dr. Carl C. Russell, superintendent of National Park Service Branch of Research and Information (July 1939). National Park Service photograph, Yellowstone Photograph Archives (YELL 34279).

the way among historians seeking a fuller and more accurate picture of just how Yellowstone came to be.

In 1948, in a short history of Yosemite National Park, historian Hans Huth referred to the campfire story as a "sentimental legend." Huth, aware of the precedents established by other preserves such as Yosemite Valley in 1864, was also aware of the pre-1870 ideas and claims of Folsom and his companions: "If things really had happened this way, it would indeed have been something of a miracle. It would have meant that public opinion had been prepared for this supposedly new and unique idea in little more than a year, and that Congress was ready to act favorably 'to set apart the vast territory of Yellowstone as a public park or pleasuring ground for the benefit and enjoyment of the people.' Ideas of such far-reaching consequence do not ripen over night; they develop slowly."[4]

By 1960, at least one National Park Service historian besides Aubrey Haines was also having strong doubts. Carl Russell, the longtime National Park Service naturalist and historian who prepared the "Madison Junction Museum Prospectus" that year, recommended against overstating the importance of the events of September 19, 1870:

> With the evidence at hand, it is hardly reasonable to assume that either the Yosemite Act of 1864 or the Yellowstone Act of 1872

16. Reenactors at Madison Campfire pageant (circa 1957–61). Jack Haynes photograph 29047 in Black Scrapbook 24 (n.p.), Yellowstone Photograph Archives.

sprang into existence full-blown and without some prior cerebration on the part of members of an earlier generation. Especially is it unrealistic (and unfair to the American people) to repeat the mistaken story regarding the Firehole birth of the National Park Idea. And I should say that it is not necessary to make such an unsupported claim in order that Yellowstone National Park may be lighted by an extra blaze of glory.[5]

But in Yellowstone, just as the campfire story was growing less trusted, new heights were reached in the official celebration of the heroism of Hedges, Langford, and their companions.

A CORNBALL PRODUCTION

In 1957, National Park Service staff began staging for the public an annual reenactment, or "pageant," of the campfire conversation with a script written by Professor Bert Hansen of the Speech and Art Department of Montana State University, Missoula. Outfitted in full frontier regalia, the actors worked their way through a twenty-three-page script, almost entirely fictional though based partially on known events, to the accompaniment of tape-recorded elk bugles and coyote calls.[6] The program was popular enough to last until 1964, but by then it had already come to the attention of Aubrey Haines, who was in the process of conducting the first thorough study of the park's complex philosophical and administrative history.

Haines was no newcomer to Yellowstone. He began his career there in December 1938 as a ranger and stayed until the late 1960s, with interruptions for service in World War II and shorter assignments in Mount Rainier National Park and Big Hole National Battlefield. Originally educated in forestry engineering and then later in history, Haines brought to his work an unusual background: his intimate acquaintance with the technical aspects of roadbuilding, architecture, and many related on-the-ground realities of running a national park, plus his long acquaintance with the Yellowstone landscape, combined with a passion for the most exacting sort of historical research. In 1960, he switched from engineering to the position of Yellowstone's first official historian, a job that he and the superintendent more or less defined as they went along.[7]

As it turned out, nothing would have a greater effect on the new historian's position than the campfire story. In June 1963, Haines sent a memo to Assistant Superintendent Richard Nelson, pointing out many

17. Reenactment of Madison Campfire Pageant at junction of Firehole and Gibbon Rivers (n.d.). National Park Service photograph (slide YNP#9182), Yellowstone Photograph Archives.

errors in the pageant script and suggesting revisions. If the pageant was "merely dramatic entertainment," he said, the errors were probably not a problem, but if it was intended as a "truly historical production," then it needed changes. Haines's own position was that "we are obliged to be strictly accurate, insofar as that is possible, *because* we are a Federal agency from which the public expects literal truth. We should not engage in dramatics *or* propaganda, as I see it."[8]

The many accuracy problems with the pageant may have been the primary reason for its demise in 1964. Or it may have been a combination of that and the dissatisfaction of actors and supervisors over the quality of the performance itself. In any case, the National Park Service correspondence relating to the campfire story from the early 1960s to the time of Yellowstone's centennial celebration in 1972 is a fascinating study of an agency struggling with self-examination. Aubrey Haines and his determined scholarly analysis were at the center of it. Professor Hansen, when informed of Haines's criticisms of the script, professed himself willing to work with him to make the necessary changes, or simply to let Haines "rewrite the whole pageant."[9] Nevertheless, the press release

18. Reenactment of Madison Campfire Pageant at junction of Firehole and Gibbon Rivers, 1960. Photograph by W. S. Keller. National Park Service photograph (slide YNP#7964). Yellowstone Photograph Archives.

announcing the 1963 pageant contained the same story, fully crediting Hedges with originating the park idea and saying that "as a direct result of their [the Washburn party's] efforts, Yellowstone was established as the first National Park in the world in 1872."[10]

The professional historians and interpreters in the agency responded with growing unease not only to the continuation of the pageant but to the very idea of the campfire story. On April 10, 1964, Chief Park Naturalist John Good, in one of the most eloquent and entertaining government memoranda we have ever encountered, took on both issues in a memorandum to Yellowstone's superintendent. Reviewing the sizable scholarly literature demonstrating that the origin of Yellowstone National Park was much more complicated than the pageant indicated, Good said, "Frankly, there is no support for the pretty picture of one altruistic mind conjuring up a breathtaking idea by a campfire on the evening of September 19, 1870." Describing the pageant not only as "dishonest" but also as a "cornball production," Good recommended that it "be dropped immediately from Yellowstone's program of activities."[11]

Throughout that year, correspondence among other specialists echoed these doubts. Charles Porter, a National Park Service historian in Washington, was said to have reached essentially the same conclusions as Haines. Edwin C. Alberts, regional chief of interpretation and visitor services, wrote that Haines's research "tends to confirm my previous suspicion that much of this was a 19th Century tourism gimmick and reinforces my long held feeling that the bland assertion attributed to Langford, et al., is apocryphal." In a message to his supervisor, Alberts again called the campfire story "apocryphal" and recommended that the agency "pull back our approach to avoid embarrassment." He said that the story could still be used "as a symbol" but that park interpreters should avoid "reference to statements made and decisions reached by the party."[12]

Some of the most intriguing and revealing deliberations, however, occurred not among the specialists but among higher administrators. The statements of Lemuel Garrison, who had been Yellowstone superintendent from 1956 until early 1964, provide an extraordinary window into the travails of a devoutly loyal National Park Service bureaucrat as he tried to come to terms with scholarly reality and, at last, surrendered to other needs. On July 10, 1964, shortly after becoming regional director of the National Park Service's Midwest Region, Garrison counseled the Yellowstone superintendent, John McLaughlin, to "proceed very cautiously and thoughtfully in our objective evaluation of a tradition of long and venerable standing. This tradition has become so entrenched, and it is such a powerful factor in dramatizing and focusing attention on the National Park concept, that we would consider it something of a calamity if it were weakened or destroyed through an overemphasis on fine shadings of historical fact."[13]

At this point in his message, Garrison exemplified the self-conscious ambivalence that some leaders of the agency suffered over this issue:

> We are aware that the last statement might seem to challenge another tradition of the Service, that is, a keen regard for historical authenticity, wherever it might lead. However, we cannot avoid a conviction in this case that the value of the tradition largely outweighs any requirements for precise documentation, or the need to require absolute scientific proof. It should be pointed out that many of our most hallowed patriotic traditions (including Paul Revere's ride, for example) must be taken on faith, rather than detailed documentation. Ideals essential to the appreciation of our

citizenship are based upon deep feelings and convictions more than documents and photographic evidence.[14]

This remarkable argument against the importance of fact was also a remarkable elevation of the campfire story into the rarified realm of America's most treasured folklore (wrong as that folklore might also be). Most of all, it is an indication of just how sacred the campfire story had become in the National Park Service.

Garrison concluded that "this matter should be considered more fully. We are entirely agreeable that Mr. Haines pursue his research as much as his conscience dictates, but we would recommend against official publication of such findings, particularly until more research and study has been given the matter."[15] Throughout the rest of Haines's National Park Service career, though there seems to have been no more formal admonition than this against the publication of his research findings, the spirit of Garrison's recommendation took a very firm hold.

On July 23, in a memorandum to the director of the National Park Service, Garrison—explaining that Charles Porter had reached conclusions similar to Haines's—again asserted that the campfire story should not be entirely jettisoned: "The campfire tradition is so important that if we did not have it we should have invented it for its fame is worldwide! Historical validity of the tradition is probably in serious doubt, but this does not reduce the value of the tradition. We should continue to emphasize it as such and capitalize on it." What makes this memorandum particularly juicy for historians is that on the carbon copy sent to Yellowstone's new superintendent, John McLaughlin, Garrison scribbled a note: "John: Horace [Albright] & others seem quite disturbed about possible effect on hallowed ground. Meanwhile, apparently Charlie Porter pursuing some subject may have come up with same conclusions. Legends are more fun than facts. LG."[16]

None of this is meant to establish Garrison as a villain in the battle over historical credibility; rather, we see him as representing the complex mixture of impulses that influenced many National Park Service staff at the time. And in the end, for all his devotion to the campfire story, he stood by Haines, as did Haines's other colleagues and supervisors in Yellowstone, who attempted to shield him from the growing furor of objections to his work. John Good, who witnessed much of this period as Haines's immediate supervisor, was "impressed with Lon Garrison in the campfire fracas. He started that damned pageant at Madison and then defended Aubrey to the end against Horace Albright and the rest of the dinosaurs."[17]

It was the agency's leadership in Washington that took the revelations about the campfire story very personally, and some were quite willing to engage Haines in debate. Others no doubt would have preferred to fire him and hear no more from anyone who shared his views. His abrupt reassignment from Yellowstone to Big Hole National Battlefield in 1964, where he served two years as management assistant (the battlefield was managed from Yellowstone at the time), was part of the price he paid for speaking out about the campfire story. Whether the transfer was accomplished by his protectors to remove him from the line of fire or by his detractors to get him out of the way, or resulted from some of both, the move took him away from Yellowstone just as his research into its history was producing solid results. (It is a testament to his resilience that he then took the opportunity to begin work on his highly regarded book about the Battle of the Big Hole.) In 1966, shortly after his return to Yellowstone, Haines remembered that "a committee which included George Baggley and Horace Albright and Lon Garrison and some others that now escape my memory, was gotten together" to reconsider the staff needs of Yellowstone, and the position of historian was abolished.[18] Sympathetic park administrators simply moved Haines into an empty geologist position, in which he continued his work until his retirement in 1969. Though the chain of events never quite yields clear cause-and-effect evidence of what now might be called harassment or retribution, the last few years of Haines's park service career seem to have been survived under a cloud of hostility.[19]

This internal conflict in the National Park Service would continue, heating up in the late 1960s and early 1970s. Thereafter it became a less pressing issue, which may account for the continued survival of so many Langford-Hedges sympathizers even today, as the agency, though quietly adjusting to the new historical perspective, never formally disavowed the story. Indeed, disavowal may not have been regarded as a reasonable option, especially in those years. Garrison's mention of "Horace" in his July 23, 1964, note to McLaughlin was an ominous signal that this issue was now well beyond the offices and hallways of the agency's leadership. It is difficult to measure the force of individual personalities in a situation like this, but the great and abiding presence of Horace Albright must

19. Horace Marden Albright (circa 1920), superintendent of Yellowstone 1919–29 and director of the National Park Service thereafter to 1933. National Park Service photograph, Yellowstone Photograph Archives.

have been important, and most people in the agency would have been reluctant to offend him.

Albright, though not a National Park Service employee after 1933, was by the 1960s one of the elder statesmen and most honored figures in the American conservation movement. His occasional visits to national parks, including Yellowstone, were events of note, like the visit of a foreign head of state. He was treated with the great deference due a man whose heroic actions had set the agency on a steady and respectable course so many years earlier. Albright, who probably learned of the challenges to the campfire story, and especially of Haines's work, during a visit to Yosemite in the 1960s, remained an ardent defender of the traditional tale until his death in 1987.[20] But he was only one of many, and it is worth turning to some representative examples of the substance of their defenses, for aside from the heat and emotion they displayed, they also asked some important questions.

Much of Albright's defense of the Langford version of the story was based on his association with the park's early protectors and explorers. In a 1984 interview he said that he actually spoke about the campfire story with people who knew the Washburn party: "I truly believe it is fact. Ever since I first went to Yellowstone in 1915, I questioned every one I could find about this very story, the old timers who were around back then, men who were around back then, men who knew the 1870 party and so forth. And I never heard so much as a deviation in the general facts. Oh, one person might have quoted Hedges this way or some other member of the party another way, but the core of the story was always the same."[21]

There is certainly some hyperbole in these statements. Albright spent little time in Yellowstone until 1919 and would have had little reason or opportunity to talk to oldtimers before that. In 1919, forty-seven years had passed since the Washburn expedition had visited Yellowstone; few (perhaps only one) of its participants were still alive. Albright seems to say that he talked not to them but to people who knew them, but he gives us no names, nothing to go on in judging how well he actually did research the story. Still, he was in Yellowstone early enough, and spent enough time with leading figures of the region, that he could well have crossed paths with some informed observers.

Albright also dismissed the possible role that Haines attributed to the railroad in the creation of the park: "I remember one time in the '20s, sitting in Glacier Park with Howard Hays and Louie Hill—you know, head of the Great Northern. Well, somehow this story came up about the Northern Pacific and Jay Cooke and Yellowstone. Way back then. Well, Louie just hooted. Said, 'Hell, if the Northern Pacific had given that much thought to it, they would have taken Yellowstone for them-selves. Wouldn't have suggested it should be a public, national park.' "[22] In light of all that several other historians have shown about the inti-mate and intricate involvement of the Northern Pacific Railroad in all of Yellowstone's early affairs, and considering what Haines specifically found about its pre-establishment role in the park, Hill's statements (and Albright's credulity) seem completely specious—hearsay based on con-jecture.[23]

The primary influence of the Northern Pacific in Yellowstone affairs from 1870 on is historical fact. As Haines pointed out, to the railroad leadership goes the distinction of making the first known mention, in writing, of the idea of turning Yellowstone into a park. An October 27, 1871, letter from A. B. Nettleton, of Jay Cooke & Co., Financial Agents, Northern Pacific Railroad Company, to Ferdinand Hayden, says that Judge William Kelley "has made a suggestion which strikes me as being an excellent one, viz.: Let Congress pass a bill reserving the Great Geyser Basin as a public park forever," and asking Hayden if he would make such a recommendation officially.[24] For this and many other reasons, Haines and other historians have long credited the railroad with significant and even driving force in the movement to establish Yellowstone National Park. It is impossible to take the protestations of Hill or Albright seriously on this point. Either Hill was being coy, or he was ignorant of the history of his own industry, and Albright was eager to believe him.

A more substantial defense of the Langford version of the campfire story came from a retired National Park Service associate director, E. T. Scoyen, who served with Albright on a centennial advisory committee that roundly defended Langford. Scoyen, writing in 1971 to the Yellowstone superintendent, Jack Anderson, actually addressed contextual issues in the respective accounts of the campfire conversation. Invoking his understanding of legal rules in evidentiary matters, he concluded that Hedges, because of his distinguished education (Yale and Harvard) and his long and honorable career in Montana, was a worthy witness and his story therefore reliable.[25]

Next, Scoyen pointed out that the other diaries, including Doane's very extensive one, were not conversational; they did not cover such things as evening gab sessions: "It would appear that the important conclusion that can be drawn here is that if the discussion took place and if he [Doane, in this case] even took personal part he would not record it. It was clearly not in accord with his method of handling his diary."[26] This is a good though not decisive point; modern expectations should not color our interpretations of what diarists might have chosen to talk about long ago. It does not, however, explain the complete absence of mention of this supposedly important park idea in the later published articles of any party member—articles that *were* conversational and often quite lengthy.

Even though conceding that the national park idea in fact did not originate at the campfire that evening (he credited Folsom with originating the idea in 1869), Scoyen maintained that it was still the case that "the park exploded into being as a result of the intense interest generated throughout the country by the reports of the sensational discoveries of the Washburn-Langford-Doane expedition."[27]

It is easy enough to follow the sequence implied by Scoyen. It was popularly assumed that because of the reports and publications of the Washburn party—most specifically a speech given by Langford in Washington early in 1871—Ferdinand Hayden, of what became the United States Geological Survey, learned of Yellowstone; official exploration and establishment thereby followed. By that line of reasoning, the Washburn party was certainly very influential, primarily through their inspiration of Hayden. This seems to have been Scoyen's point, but it raises two distinct issues here. The first is whether or not Hayden was already familiar with reports of Yellowstone's geothermal and scenic wonders when he heard Langford's speech. The second is whether or not Langford's speech influenced Hayden's decision to take his survey to Yellowstone.

First, we now know that Hayden *had* learned of Yellowstone and its reported wonders at least fourteen years earlier than Langford's speech. As Marlene Deahl Merrill stated in *Yellowstone and the Great West* (1999), "Ferdinand Hayden first heard 'wonderful tales' about the Yellowstone Basin from Jim Bridger in 1856, when they both served on a survey that explored northeast of what is today's park under the command of Lieutenant Gouverneur Kemble Warren."[28] (This statement should not, however, be misunderstood as placing Hayden close to present Yellowstone National Park in 1856; the Warren party ascended the Yellowstone River only as far as the mouth of the Powder River in eastern Montana.) Then, in 1860, Hayden was a member of an expedition under Captain William F. Raynolds that approached the Yellowstone Plateau from the southeast and was turned back from the extreme headwaters of the Yellowstone River by snow.[29] Again, Bridger was a member of the party, and again, Hayden would have had abundant opportunity to hear tales of Yellowstone's wonders. As well, Aubrey Haines has pointed out that Hayden was later told of the peculiar features of Yellowstone by acting governor of Montana Territory, Thomas Meagher, and Father Kuppens when he met those men in the Helena area.[30] There seems no question, then, that Hayden had long known of Yellowstone, probably even before Langford himself had heard of it.

As for Langford's speech having had an effect on Hayden's plans, recent scholars are skeptical. Hayden's biographer Mike Foster refers to it as "mythology" and traces the idea's rise in popularity through the writings of several historians, all of whom relied on incomplete and unconvincing evidence. (Foster points out that it is sometimes difficult to determine Hayden's plans and motivations during his years of survey work because in the intense competition among the great western surveys, Hayden was quite secretive about his plans from year to year.) We agree with the case that Hayden's biographers Foster and James Cassidy make against Langford's speech having had any meaningful influence on the plans of Ferdinand Hayden.[31]

Even if there were a more direct cause-and-effect relationship between the Washburn party and the activities of Hayden and other park promoters leading to the establishment of the park, such a sequence leaves out far too much, including the complex motivations of the Washburn party and the behind-the-scenes role of the railroad. But complexities of this kind were apparently not tolerable to Scoyen, whose closing argument eloquently, perhaps definitively, resorted to the core sentiments of all lovers of the campfire story, making it clear that this was an emotional rather than merely an intellectual issue:

> This campfire and the discussion which took place there is a great story and one of the significant events of National Park History. It is an old and revered tradition firmly believed by thousands of people who have labored over the years in the field of National Parks. It places the birth of the *movement* towards establishing the first National Park with a wonderful and interesting group of rugged western pioneers. It relates to an outstanding example of unselfish citizenship for the public good. It has been pointed out as such in thousands of lectures in halls and around hundreds of campfires. I ever found a source of inspiration, while performing my tasks in the parks over the nearly half-century I served, in the story of the Madison Junction campfire. I, for one, will not be satisfied with mere confirmation as a reason for throwing this valuable National Park asset out the window or degrading it in any way.[32]

In other words, it is a true story not only because the evidence is adequate but also because those who love it need it to be true.

Perhaps the most engaging and best-informed attempt to challenge Haines came from Ronald Lee, special assistant to the director, in 1971 and 1972 as Haines was struggling to prepare his monumental history, *The Yellowstone Story*, for publication. Having read the portions (about forty pages) of the manuscript relating to the campfire story, Lee prepared a series of letters and critiques addressing a number of issues that appeared in the draft manuscript. These complex and detailed remarks involved challenges relating to some specific criticisms Haines had made of Langford, and of Chittenden's handling of information given him by Langford.

The exchange of letters between Haines and Lee, and other National Park Service personnel, primarily involved disagreement over the relative significance of various parties in the creation of Yellowstone National Park. Lee generally found Langford more trustworthy than Haines did.

20. *Comic strip panels related to 1870 Washburn expedition campfire from Bill Chapman's* Yarns of the Yellowstone *(1972), published for the park's hundredth anniversary. Yellowstone National Park Research Library, Rare Separates file. Courtesy Bill Chapman.*

Lee wondered, for example, if Langford were as unworthy and self-promoting as Haines believed, and willing to fabricate the campfire story, why he would place someone else (Hedges) rather than himself in the starring role.[33]

Haines, though, did not regard the campfire conversation as a complete fabrication. He thought it had occurred in some form, but he was trying to place it in accurate context as only one of many events leading to the creation of the park. As for Langford's giving Hedges the credit, Haines maintained that Langford's entire career was made up of such maneuvers, that he was "never more than a coat-tail rider, dependent on family and friends for the influence which got him jobs and favors. He can easily be suspected of hungering for glory and ready enough to claim a share of it—by advancing the idea that he called for the establishment of a Yellowstone National Park while on his lecture tour in the East."[34]

Both Lee and Haines presented much contextual evidence; their differences often came down to how much they were willing to trust any of the historical characters involved (Lee, for example, was much impressed by Langford's letter to Albert Matthews, quoted in chapter 3). And although we are consistently inclined to find Haines's arguments more persuasive, we must recognize that such judgments are always ultimately inconclusive. Haines and Lee both acknowledged that a central feature of the campfire story, and of competing views of it, was the question of who should get credit for the creation of Yellowstone National Park. By the time Langford published his *Diary*, many a claimant had come forth, or had been put forth by friends, as the most important person in the process. It seems beyond doubt that none of these contestants ultimately proved more capable of putting his name forward with questionable justification than did Nathaniel Langford, and none of the others was more retiring in the face of promotion of his name by others than was Cornelius Hedges. Their relative merits aside, together Langford and Hedges were still, in the minds of many, a powerful and symbolic team, one not to be discarded lightly. By questioning their version of the campfire story, Haines had taken on some of the strongest, most determined, and perhaps even vindictive forces in the National Park Service. Careful historical scholarship was not going to be enough to keep him going.

CHAPTER EIGHT

It Came Out All Right!

The approach of the park's centennial (1972) compelled National Park Service managers to pay close attention to the debate over the Madison campfire story. Some, especially Ronald Lee, urged that the story be a centerpiece of the celebration as it had been fifty years earlier, whereas Haines stood firm on his historical interpretations.

This situation has great potential for oversimplification. At first glance it is easy to stereotype the two positions: you have your stodgy ideologues in charge of the agency, and your bravely principled rebel challenging authority and tradition. No doubt both stodginess and bravery were involved, and without question, vindictiveness against Haines was one result. But as in any such controversy, a broad spectrum of positions developed. Even among the most thoughtful defenders of the old story (who were in many cases also the most powerful), there is relatively little of the almost willful deceit we now perceive in Lemuel Garrison's remark (quoted in chapter 7) that the story should be used whether it was true or not. And in fairness we must wonder to what extent Garrison was joking, or being cynically humorous; after all, he became a staunch defender of Haines when the historian was attacked for his views.

In fact, most park service traditionalists, though indeed offended by this threat to their beloved campfire story, were also sincerely convinced that Haines's new interpretations needed simply to be dealt with cautiously. They made a point that many of us would probably make under similar circumstances—that as with any major revision of an important historical episode, sorting it all out would take some time. Every scholar, no matter how distinguished, must accept that the judgment of his or her peers takes time. But for the leadership of Yellowstone and of the National Park Service, time was short. Events conspired to press a formal

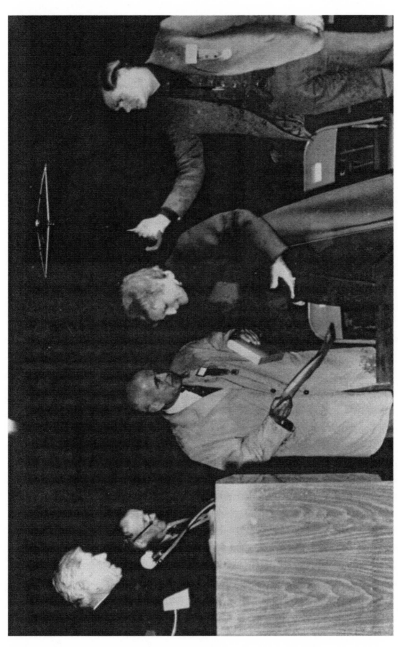

21. *Mrs. Richard M. Nixon, representing President Richard Nixon, accepting a gift from Secretary of the Interior Rogers Morton (far left) at celebration of Yellowstone's hundredth anniversary, Madison Junction. National Park Service photograph, Yellowstone Photograph Archives (YELL 114783-2).*

22. *Yellowstone Historian "Emeritus" Aubrey L. Haines, teaching his course "Northern Roadside History of Yellowstone National Park" (August 1, 1994). Photograph by M. A. Bellingham, Yellowstone Photograph Archives.*

resolution to an issue that under other circumstances might have settled into a long, slow debate.

As 1972 approached, planners scheduled the dedication of a plaque at Madison Junction as part of the Yellowstone centennial celebration, to be held in conjunction with the Second World Conference on National Parks. The text of the plaque became a sore point, and its wording was decided upon only after Robert Utley, the chief historian of the National Park Service, stepped in. Lee, in his campaign to make sure the plaque supported the traditional campfire story, took the hard line that Hedges must be acknowledged as the originator of the Yellowstone Park idea. No one had to ask Haines (who had by then retired) what he thought of that; his opposition to the story was clear. Utley was called upon to sort out this heated and very touchy matter.[1]

By this time, on the eve of the centennial, there was even more at stake for Haines, and for historical scholarship, than getting the National Park Service to accept a more guarded and defensible version of the events that led to the creation of Yellowstone National Park. Haines had two important books essentially completed, both significant contributions to Yellowstone history and both addressing the park's creation. As part of his work as Yellowstone's historian in the 1960s, Haines had prepared a massive two-volume record that covered the entire sweep of Yellowstone's human history, from the long residence of Native peoples through

23. *Robert Utley, historian (n.d.), office shot with painting of Grand Canyon of Yellowstone. National Park Service photograph, Harpers Ferry Center.*

Euro-American exploration and the administrative history of the park. This was the manuscript that was to become *The Yellowstone Story*, which he finished writing about 1969, the year of his retirement. But following his retirement, Haines was commissioned by the National Park Service to produce a one-volume documentary history of the area up to the date of the park's establishment. This work became *Yellowstone National Park: Its Exploration and Establishment*, a book featuring numerous extended firsthand accounts of the park and the adventure of its creation.

Haines's presentation in these books of his case against Langford's campfire story served as the most formal scholarly notice yet presented to the National Park Service that the story needed reconsideration. Utley, then as now one of the most influential and prominent of western historical scholars, had stepped into the middle of a complicated and delicate situation. He was not only mediating an internal agency debate; he was in effect conducting a peer review on portions of Haines's book manuscripts—two of the most significant new works of historical scholarship to be produced by the National Park Service in many years. Utley's own recollection of sorting out the problem was recently published as part of his tribute memorializing the career of Aubrey Haines:

> And thus was I, as chief historian of the National Park Service, drawn into the fray. I delved into the matter and satisfied myself that Aubrey was right, that Langford had contrived the campfire scene in an embellished or wholly fabricated diary published thirty-four years after the fact. Langford's duplicity had imbued Aubrey Haines with a genuine loathing for the man. As the 1972 centennial of Yellowstone approached, the park service commissioned Aubrey, retired and living in Bozeman, Montana, to prepare a documentary history of the exploration and establishment of the park. The drafts that I reviewed in Washington set off alarm bells, for I knew that his rough handling of Langford would stir up trouble and interfere with publication.
>
> Hence my journey in February 1971, with my deputy A. Russell Mortensen, to Bozeman and a long negotiation around Aubrey's kitchen table. I told him I would go all the way in backing his demolition of the legend if he would call off his personal vendetta against Langford and let the evidence speak for itself. Not too happily, he agreed, and the book finally found its way into print in 1974, two years late.[2]

As for the plaque that Lee insisted pay specific tribute to Hedges, Utley's influence resulted in a somewhat milder statement:

THE FIRST NATIONAL PARK

Here at the junction of the Firehole and Gibbon Rivers on September 19, 1870, members of the Washburn-Langford-Doane Expedition gathered around a campfire the last evening of their historic exploration of the Yellowstone country and discussed the astounding natural wonders they had seen. There emerged an idea, expressed by Cornelius Hedges, that there should be no private ownership of these wonders but that the area should be preserved for public enjoyment. Others shared these views, and on

March 1, 1872, President Ulysses S. Grant signed the Act establishing Yellowstone as the world's first national park. In the century since, 1200 national parks and equivalent preserves have been established by more than 90 nations.

Dedicated during the Second World Conference on National Parks[,] September 18–27, 1972

It is remarkable to us that, as generous as this statement was to the traditionalists' viewpoint, it was considered at the time to be a very toned-down version of what they wanted the plaque to say. It seems certain that it was a significant disappointment to Ronald Lee.

Utley's important influence on the wording prevented the National Park Service from presenting a baldly inaccurate story on the plaque. "Others shared these views" indicated that the park originated from a broader effort than that mounted by members of the Washburn party. The vague statement that the Washburn party wanted the area to be "preserved for public enjoyment" replaced the belief that they had specified a "national park." Nor does the plaque name Hedges as the first ever to have this idea; it says only that Hedges "expressed it" on this night.

These equivocations must have been hard for the traditionalists to swallow. But when we exercise the luxury of hindsight, it seems to us that for all its equivocations and caution, the text of the plaque was still a generous capitulation to the problematic opinions of the supporters of the traditional campfire tale. True, Haines's more sophisticated view of the events surrounding the creation of the park did eventually prevail. True, the flawed story that the plaque more or less implies has largely faded from the campfire programs that interpretive rangers present nightly only a few yards away at the Madison Campground amphitheater. But as long as that simplistic old tale lingers in such durable forms as this plaque, it seems to us that the accurate interpretation of Yellowstone's history will be somewhat compromised.

The eventual fate of the campfire story in the agency may best be exemplified by yet another attempt to memorialize the Washburn party. In July 1972 the site of the campfire was proposed for the National Register of Historic Places, in a nomination written by Yellowstone's chief park naturalist, William Dunmire, and Donald Dosch of the Midwest Regional Office. The nomination was endorsed by the appropriate offices in the state of Wyoming, slipped into procedural limbo, then reemerged in 1977, when it briefly seemed to be on track again. But by early 1978, almost certainly because of the growing doubts about the historical reliability of the campfire conversation (and perhaps also because it was a low priority), the proposal seemed to have been quietly shelved.[3] As so often appears to happen in large institutions, a policy, program, or belief may fade from view for complicated reasons having as much to do with lack of interest as with formal disapproval.

Regrettably, however, the same sort of treatment was given to Haines's completed manuscript history of Yellowstone, originally intended to be published in time for the centennial in 1972. As explained by Utley, publication of Haines's one-volume documentary history, *Yellowstone National Park: Its Exploration and Establishment*, was delayed until 1974, when the U.S. Government Printing Office produced a workmanlike edition. Although it had a fairly limited distribution, it immediately assumed an important place in Yellowstone historical scholarship alongside Richard Bartlett's *Nature's Yellowstone*, which appeared the same year and covered essentially the same pre-establishment period in a thoroughly researched but less documentary narrative.[4]

But Haines's monumental book *The Yellowstone Story* just sat, year after year, wrangled over and in danger of oblivion. His recollections of this period were pointed and critical:

> I had completed and submitted that manuscript before retiring in 1969—it was to be available in printed form for the Centennial Year; but, instead, it began a long Hegira through many hands in the Washington Office and seemed destined to die of old age there without approval. A copy of Ronald Lee's unkind letter reached me late in 1971, and I could see from it that the problem was official disapproval of my handling of the "campfire story." So I wrote Utley, defending my viewpoint. . . . That led to some lame attempts to soften my attitude and theirs without getting anywhere, and then to an attempt to emasculate the manuscript by having a Washington Office editor cut it down to a single-book size. I finally balked and asked that the manuscript be returned to Yellowstone Park, which was done—five years lost for no good reason![5]

It is unclear now to what extent "emasculation" was an actual aim of the Washington office at this point. Utley, in his correspondence with Lee in 1972, made it clear that he was going to stand behind Haines's most controversial interpretations.[6] Yellowstone staff had the impression that the manuscript was being condensed primarily because there was doubt that a two-volume history of the park would have sufficient marketability. But it seems certain that whatever the motivations behind the proposed abridgment of the big book, one effect certainly would have been that any individual topic would get a lighter and less detailed discussion. Such a consequence would almost have to work against Haines's analysis of the campfire story, even if the editor had no specific orders to "cleanse" the text of controversy.

Fortunately, by the 1970s, Yellowstone's staff were just as reluctant as was Haines to see his great opus undergo extreme condensation. After its return to Yellowstone from Washington, the manuscript resided in the park's research library for a few years and was used only lightly (by us, among others) until the mid-1970s. Then, Yellowstone's chief and assistant chief of interpretation, Alan Mebane and John Tyers, along with the leadership of the Yellowstone Library and Museum Association (YLMA, now the Yellowstone Association), decided that it was too important to remain unpublished any longer. Though some park staff were still unsure of the marketability of the full manuscript, there was no apparent resistance to retaining Haines's revision of the campfire story. So after an eager, well-credentialed publisher, Colorado Associated University Press, took an interest, and its director, John Schwartz, expressed confidence that the full work would do fine in the marketplace, publication was achieved cooperatively by the press and YLMA in 1977. Late that year, YLMA—along with Haines's friends and former colleagues in the National Park Service, led by Yellowstone Superintendent John Townsley—hosted a community party in the historic Fort Yellowstone "canteen" at Mammoth Hot Springs to celebrate the book's appearance.[7]

In this way, *The Yellowstone Story* finally emerged from obscurity to acclaim and broad acceptance as a foundation document of Yellowstone historical scholarship, belying fears that it would be too long to appeal to park enthusiasts. Even at 928 pages, a quarter-century after its first appearance it continues to sell, entertain, and educate. In fact, we believe that its success is in good part due to the thoroughness that its size allows. Yellowstone's serious enthusiasts long ago demonstrated a passion for the finest details of the park's remarkable saga, and these two volumes fuel that passion well. It is our opinion that *The Yellowstone Story* is the single most important book ever published about Yellowstone National Park.

That the park's friends were almost denied access to it just because of an in-house quarrel over the interpretations in a few of its pages still amazes and appalls us.

It is an odd footnote to this tale of embattled scholarship that the very reason for the delay in publication of *The Yellowstone Story* hardly survived in Haines's final manuscript anyway. In its published version, as well as in the earlier single-volume book, Haines voluntarily chose at last to deal with the campfire story in muted terms. Indeed, after successfully surviving the bitter attacks of his critics, he so toned down his critical interpretation of the campfire story that the doubts and questions he had raised during the years of prepublication debate are almost invisible to the casual reader. In his memorial tribute to Haines in 2000, Bob Utley expressed disappointment that in *Yellowstone National Park: Its Exploration and Establishment* Haines seemed to have *over*reacted to his counsel that he calm his attacks on Langford:

> Aubrey took me too seriously. I wanted him to deal with the camp-fire tale in a dispassionate analysis of the evidence. Instead, he al-most entirely ignored it, truly letting the evidence speak for itself. A few gentle hints prompted the informed reader to look more closely at the documents, but nowhere did he state explicitly that the campfire scenario finds no support in credible evidence. I wish he had discussed the issue as I had urged, so that it could stand be-fore the world truly disposed of by the preeminent expert on the subject. Curiously, a two-volume opus [i.e., *The Yellowstone Story*], published by a university press three years later, afforded him the chance to set the record straight without outside influence. He did not. Perhaps in truth he was just weary of fighting.[8]

Happily, the delayed publication of *The Yellowstone Story* and Aubrey's low-key retelling of the campfire story did not hinder the continued reconsideration of Langford and his tale of altruistic explorers. Haines, who had done his homework well, was part of an intellectual community that included other historical scholars. Interest in conservation history was growing, and Yellowstone received its share of attention. In *How the U.S. Cavalry Saved Our National Parks* (1971), the historian H. D. Hampton reviewed pre-1870 proposals to make Yellowstone a park. He called the National Park Service's annual reenactments of the campfire at Madison Junction in the late 1950s and early 1960s a "travesty," pointing out that "the park idea did not originate in the Yellowstone area, but in the act of Congress in 1864 granting the Yosemite Valley to the State of California."[9] Hampton's analysis of the situation appropriately stressed the complex and diffuse nature of the social and political processes by which Yellowstone National Park was established. Like Haines, he emphasized the parallels between Yosemite and Yellowstone within the rise of the park movement.

Introduction of Yosemite into dialogues over the origin of Yellowstone adds another important element of complexity to the conversation. Throughout the long history of the national parks a good-natured rivalry has flourished between the two "Y-Parks" over which was actually "first" in any sense. The set of players and advocates involved in the establishment of the first Yosemite reserve thus must be considered in any complete analysis of the complex patrimony of Yellowstone National Park.

Richard Bartlett, one of the past century's most important scholars of Yellowstone history, likewise dealt firmly with the campfire story in *Nature's Yellowstone* (1974). He spoke skeptically of Langford's blatant self-promotion, describing him as "the man who would most especially have liked mankind to give him credit for being the prime mover." Like Hampton but in much more detail, Bartlett ably traced the various forces and individuals involved in the creation of the park. Like Haines he gave Hedges and Langford relatively little credit, and like Haines and Hampton he recognized the powerful presence of the Northern Pacific Railroad in the park movement. With justifiable sarcasm he repeatedly diminished Langford's stature. Reviewing the contemporary accounts of the 1870 expedition members, Bartlett pointed out that they said nothing about the campfire conversation, "yet in 1904 it was presented as the most exciting event of the expedition after leaving the geysers. The campfire legend has grown over the years. Langford saw to it that a plaque was erected at the site; the National Park Service in later years added to the myth by presenting a pageant there about the whole affair."[10]

Reconsideration of the campfire story has continued ever since, both within and beyond the National Park Service. In 1992 a park service historian, Richard Sellars, while researching the history of natural resource management in the national parks, gave the campfire story another working over. He concluded, like so many before him, that although it is impossible to know exactly what did occur that night at Madison Junction, many other forces were obviously involved in the creation of the park, and one of the most influential was certainly the commercial interest of the Northern Pacific Railroad.[11]

24. *Madison Junction Amphitheater with National Park Mountain in the background (1976). National Park Service photograph, Yellowstone Photograph Archives (YELL 95082).*

Much of the era of controversy over the campfire story is within the memories of the authors of this book, each of whom has been actively involved in Yellowstone historical study for nearly thirty years. Schullery recalls that when he first worked in Yellowstone as a seasonal ranger-naturalist in 1972, the campfire story was widely known to be spurious or at least suspect but was still invoked on official, ceremonial occasions. Whittlesey remembers hearing ranger-naturalists tell the story uncritically during the first years he worked in Yellowstone, 1969 to 1972, and wondering why Bartlett's 1974 book seemed to discredit Langford but the park staff did not. It appeared most likely that seasonal employees, who were unlikely to be informed of touchy issues, were just slow to get the word that the campfire story had been called into question.

The story was indeed fading, but it existed in a dynamic atmosphere rather like that of the new rule that visitors were no longer allowed to feed the black bears. There were a few rangers still willing to tell the campfire story; there were a few rangers still willing to let people feed bears; and there was still sufficient unofficial sanction of both behaviors to let them happen. Both the campfire story and the bear feeding were wrong, but both were also venerable institutions, irresistible to the tradition-bound, the optimistically sympathetic, and the lazy.

The brightest note we can offer about this slow, painful process of revision involves Aubrey Haines himself. It is informal consensus among park staff who remember the controversy that its cost to Aubrey was high: there were unwritten, unofficial calls for his head, the strongest often offered by the least well informed.[12] It must have been a very difficult period even for so determined and careful a scholar, but in the last years of his life he looked back on it, and on the eventual success of his campaign for a more accurate portrayal of Yellowstone history, with an admirable forbearance. He repeatedly expressed his gratitude to the entire Yellowstone administration and all his coworkers, as well as to the community of historical scholars in the National Park Service, for their support and protection during the worst days of the controversy. Though the debate and its effects had to be a painful and miserable experience, Aubrey struggled to maintain what we found to be an admirable sense of proportion about what he lost, as well as what he gained, in fighting such a nasty battle:

> It cost me my historian position and that caused me to retire early, but that wasn't all bad. I continued to work on Yellowstone's his-

tory, and on other good projects, from the basis of a secure retirement (I am in the twenty-ninth year of that retirement now), so
I don't see that they hurt me much. Frankly, I was sustained by
the fact that Yellowstone Park supported me—put me in the then
open position of Naturalist-Geologist, George Marler's slot, va-
cated by his retirement—so I could finish The Yellowstone Story
after my historian position was terminated. The NPS historians in
Region II and the Washington Office (Mattes, Tompson, Appel-
man, Utley and Mattison) were supportive and helpful. It came
out all right![13]

Haines wrote these words in 1998 and continued to believe them until
his death, on September 10, 2000.

Among the opinions, ideas, and advice offered us by readers of manuscript versions of this book, the most forceful criticism was that we have
been too kind. We were told that in our desire to be fair to all parties in
the original events and all disputants in the ensuing controversy, we have
taken too much of the punch from our argument that the campfire story
is false, or have been too easy on the people who attempted to discredit
Aubrey Haines.

Perhaps this criticism is accurate. After all, the evidence convinces
us that Nathaniel Langford behaved shamefully in his treatment of the
Yellowstone historical record. And we still become angry, after all these
years, when we think of how Aubrey Haines was treated by certain distant
officials in the National Park Service. So we may indeed be guilty of
overcaution or meekness in our judgments.

But then, it is probably past time that some participant in a Yellowstone controversy is guilty of being too polite. Certainly, we do not
want to be guilty of the rhetorical excesses and embarrassingly careless
thinking that characterized most of the defense of the campfire story.
And after all, if Aubrey Haines himself could be so forgiving, we might
be wise to follow his example.

CHAPTER NINE

Leaving It All Behind

Aubrey Haines's careful dismantling of the Madison campfire story in the 1960s and 1970s might now be seen as an early episode in a wholesale reconsideration of the history and character of national parks. That reconsideration has continued ever since and, in all respects, has greatly increased our appreciation for the complexity of the historical process of park creation and management through the years. Even more, it has vastly heightened our appreciation for all the things that a national park can mean to the world. Most to the point of this book, it has made debates over the specific events of the Madison campfire seem ever less relevant.

The long investigation into the Madison campfire myth is typical of the scholarly reaction against any idealized, self-congratulatory notion of how human society works. A particularly telling, if still controversial, example of that reaction was offered by another Haines contemporary, historian Alfred Runte, whose *National Parks: The American Experience* (1979) also highlighted the flaws in Langford's story. Runte proposed at least two factors that further complicated the simplistic story presented by Langford. For one, Runte pointed out that Congress, before designating public lands as national parks, had to be persuaded that those lands were "worthless" for other purposes.[1] Thus, the willingness to behave altruistically was contingent upon the impossibility of commerce. Historians have quarreled over this "worthless lands" hypothesis ever since Runte offered it, and we remain uncertain just how significant a factor it was in congressional debates over Yellowstone.[2] But merely by pointing out that discussion of the point arose whenever a park was proposed, Runte injected some much-needed skepticism into the study of park origination.

Runte's second such contribution was his suggestion that American national parks were created in part because of "cultural insecurity" on the part of Americans; they were, according to this line of reasoning, an answer to the architectural and cultural wonders of the Old World, a means of establishing a national pride of place.[3] Runte was making an important point. There is an abundance of documentary evidence that early visitors to American national parks compared the features they saw to Old World (and New World, for that matter) architecture and sought cultural connections with natural features. There is also ample indication that many parks provided visitors with a sense of patriotic pride and thus elevated the American citizenry's opinions of itself relative to the Old World. No doubt American parks still serve these purposes. We are not convinced that these things were a significant or even minor factor in the creation of Yellowstone National Park. But again, Runte advanced the dialogues over what it takes to cause a park to appear. American society was not simpleminded in 1872 and did not function independently of the rest of the world. The Washburn party was not independent of the planet that night. Not only did Yellowstone result from changing attitudes toward nature in the nineteenth century; it was born into a global society in which nations watched each other with admiration, animosity, and envy.

But Runte's work, like Haines's, was symptomatic of larger, far-reaching reconsiderations of how and why public lands wind up being protected—not only how it happens and why we want it done but even such fundamental questions as whether our notion of protection makes sense in the first place. Though some of the best examples of this reconsideration have involved Yellowstone, it is a process that has affected the entire realm of public lands management in the United States.

When Aubrey Haines was conducting his study of Yellowstone's history, about the time of the passage of the Wilderness Act of 1964, most people still saw national parks and similar wilderness areas as fairly simple both in their character and in their mission.[4] They were set aside to preserve pristine examples of the American landscape; what could be more sensible, or easier to achieve? Except for fears of overuse by an adoring public, such lands had their future sorted out and their sense of direction well in hand. But even as Haines burrowed into various archives and libraries to clarify the details of Yellowstone history, other scholars were puzzling out issues that would soon come to the attention of Yellowstone's managers, friends, and constituencies. Among these was the realization that the very notion of a pristine wilderness was problematic.

It was problematic culturally, because humans had occupied and used

74

these lands for thousands of years before they were suddenly "preserved" as wilderness. Early national park proponents thought it was enough to keep them in much the same condition they had been in when first visited by Euro-Americans, with no awareness, much less regard, for the many effects of earlier occupants. Native peoples, through their aggressive use of fire, their hunting and gathering practices, and even their agriculture had in many cases significantly altered these landscapes, even selectively maintaining portions of them in certain conditions for certain purposes. Creating "wilderness" in such already occupied lands had a variety of consequences only poorly appreciated by most professional ecologists and managers and not understood at all by the general public.[5]

The implications of an awareness of anthropogenic influences in shaping park landscapes have not been lost on national park scholars. Theodore Catton, in *Inhabited Wilderness* (1997), and Mark Spence, in *Dispossessing the Wilderness* (1999), are among many scholars whose work provides broad-ranging critiques of the uneasy relationship that modern national park management has with the pre-Euro-American past.[6] Spence, for example, deals with Yellowstone managers' early removal of Native people from the park area and subsequent denial of their access to traditionally used park lands and resources:

> Yellowstone also provides the first example of removing a native population in order to "preserve" nature. As an empty, seemingly untouched landscape, locked away and undiscovered for centuries, Yellowstone represents a perfect Eden, a virtual manifestation of God's original design for America. This conception of wilderness preceded the creation of the first national park by a number of years and proved so powerful that early preservationists either dismissed or ignored any evidence of native use and habituation. And later, when park officials did take notice of Indians, they viewed native hunters as a dangerous and unnatural threat to Yellowstone's fragile environment—even when government surveys demonstrated that populations of most game animals in the park continued to increase through the late nineteenth and early twentieth centuries. These ideas shaped park policy for three decades, until Yellowstone had indeed become a place that native people neither used nor occupied.[7]

Though it is an overstatement that early park protectors "dismissed or ignored any evidence of native use and habitation" (Philetus Norris, Yellowstone's second superintendent, 1877–82, officially published at length on the park's extensive archaeological resources, for example), there was without question a pronounced tendency to regard Indian impact on the Yellowstone landscape as either bad or inappropriate. The distinction must be made between admitting that Indians had effects on the landscape (an admission many early inhabitants no doubt were willing to make, even if they did not fully comprehend the effects) and admitting that those effects were good and important or somehow constituted proof of native rights to continue using park landscapes (an admission virtually no early park protector would have made).

Also, as thoughtless and cruel as whites were in removing Native peoples from ancestral lands, one must be careful about ascribing too complex a motivation to those whites. For example, as Joseph Weixelman has demonstrated in his study of the popular white belief that Indians were afraid of the geyser basins, the dominant white culture was happy, even eager, to believe that Indians had little use for the Yellowstone area.[8] But it remains somewhat questionable that this belief was motivated by a need for excuses to exclude Indians from Yellowstone. The sad truth is that whites of that time were inclined simply to take what they wanted from Indians; they hardly needed sophisticated reasoning or anthropological support to do so.

These complications in interpreting the historical record of the disenfranchisement of Indians aside, the emergence of this more complicated view of national park landscapes as places of longtime human occupation and manipulation has profound implications for an understanding of the origins of Yellowstone. The Madison campfire story indeed told us of preserving a sort of Eden. Langford and his companions, like most of their contemporaries, had a whitewashed, simplistic view of this wild landscape, and Native people were without question not going to be a part of its imagined future. In a peculiarly ironic twist to the story, Langford's own goal for Yellowstone, which he attempted to characterize as purely altruistic, would in fact eventually be judged not only exclusionary and greedy but also racist.

The creation story of Yellowstone National Park reveals further complications in Spence's comments about the way that "populations of most game animals in the park continued to increase through the late nineteenth and early twentieth centuries."[9] Spence here took the simplistic and still unproven position that the exclusion of Indians led to an overpopulation of native wildlife (which ceased to be "game animals" when hunting was outlawed in the park in 1883). But it is certainly true that the population sizes and trends of Yellowstone's large mammals constitute a central issue in the ongoing dialogues concerning management of the park. And though it is also true that any consideration of the historic size of native Yellowstone wildlife populations absolutely must involve possible Native human influences, for the purposes of this book we must address issues perhaps more ecological than cultural.

Through much of the twentieth century the idea of wilderness was quite simple in the public mind. At the time of the creation of Yellowstone in 1872 and of the National Park Service in 1916, large natural settings were still generally thought of as benign and tending toward a stable state in which nothing much surprising happened.[10] Establishing a national park, then, was simply a matter of deciding on boundaries; nature, widely perceived as a stability-loving force, would take care of the rest. But as ecologists have come to recognize the inherent and often unpredictable flexibility of ecosystems, in which plants and animals experience complex and still inscrutable shifts in abundance and distribution on the landscape, the idea of the national park as Langford envisioned it in his Madison campfire story has become less and less a valid part of modern management.

With or without Native human influences, with or without the manipulations of Euro-American managers, wild ecological systems constantly do surprising and alarming things. Scores of scientific studies in Yellowstone in the past forty years have affirmed that climate, fire, predation, herbivory, erosion, and other ongoing processes are capable of dramatically reshaping the wild setting.[11] Such books as Mary Meagher's *The Bison of Yellowstone National Park* (1973), Douglas Houston's *The Northern Yellowstone Elk* (1982), Paul Schullery's *Searching for Yellowstone* (1997), and James Pritchard's *Preserving Yellowstone's Natural Conditions* (1999) document the long, halting course of management from the time of Langford's simplistic notions of the park to today's contentious, multilayered idea of Yellowstone as a world-class laboratory for the study of ecology—a view which, Pritchard demonstrates, surfaced in the early 1900s and has struggled for respect ever since.[12] As Pritchard summarized it:

> We sometimes think of nature preservation in the parks as the direct descendant of aesthetic preservation. In fact, a complex interaction among cultural movements, ideal notions about how nature

works, changing conservation strategies, scientific information, institutional structures, and a good dose of politics has informed and shaped park policies. The scientists' proposal during the early twentieth century that Yellowstone serve as an ecological control has endured as one of the most significant purposes for the national parks, underlying both management and public understandings of nature in Yellowstone.[13]

The Yellowstone National Park that Langford claimed to envision at the Madison campfire and that he later managed as first superintendent was an institution essentially devoid of any commitment or concern for such complex ecological issues.

Both naturally and culturally, then, national park landscapes spent the twentieth century putting their managers through a painful field course in what nature really does when "set aside." Moreover, the mixture of nature and culture in our evolving concept of national parks and similar reserves has brought about further tensions, and further movement away from the simple idea behind the original Yellowstone National Park. As generations of managers have confronted local ecological issues, the lines between nature and culture have become blurred. For example, some observers wonder if national parks and similar reserves are themselves just huge cultural constructs; for some people, denying these landscapes the human influences that acted upon them for so many centuries has lessened their authenticity. Critics and opponents of wilderness preservation have been especially attracted to the rhetoric of the wilderness area as an ironically artificial landscape, bereft of some of the most important influences that shaped it over the millennia. And they have been loud in their criticism of the "wilderness myth."[14]

Advocates of wilderness preservation have at the same time celebrated the special value of such areas because of their separation from human influence—which seems to them proportionately more important as there is less such land on earth. Among the interesting points implicit in this position is that there is an actual advantage to be had in completely excluding the influence even of Native peoples: the only way to truly understand how wild ecosystems function is by watching them do so with as little human intervention, Native or otherwise, as possible; otherwise, constantly confusing human effects with those of other forces will prevent the sensible management not only of these lands but of others.[15]

Not surprisingly, many strongly expressed variations on these opinions have arisen about the "right" way to deal with "preserved" lands in light of all these new revelations. One need only read the articles and editorial pages of Yellowstone-area newspapers for a few weeks to discover that the modern regional landscape is heavily populated with people who are almost religiously confident that they know exactly the best way to manage the park and other public lands. These people agree on nothing except that it is not being done correctly now.

The idea that the national park might be a highly volatile institution, redefined by each succeeding generation, would not have occurred to Langford. Few people in his day had any notion of the complexity of ecological and cultural effects on a landscape, and even today most of the public (and at least some of the congressional leadership in whose hands lies the fate of the parks) probably see parks much the way Langford did. But that simplistic view betrays what the parks have become: great experimental laboratories in which to test ideas of nature and culture and how they connect.

All this contention and the strongly expressed opinions about the "right" way to "solve the problems" of the park suggest a widespread conviction that there is a perfect way to manage Yellowstone. There seems to be a public confidence that, though we may be off track at any given time, parks are heading toward the state of perfection that most people probably thought Yellowstone had already achieved in 1872. But as geographer Judith Meyer has complained,

> Scholars writing about the evolution of the national parks or the national park ideal are often guilty of operating under the assumption that there is an "ideal" national park. They intimate that the evolution of the national parks has proceeded with an inherent determinism—along with science and broadening ecological awareness—from a less-than-noble state toward a more perfect national park ideal or goal in nature preservation. And, the phrase "the national park ideal" is commonly used to describe the end-product of a complex and varied history of national interests in nature preservation. Such thinking and terminology create the illusion that there is, indeed, one ideal or set of values to which all parks should conform and that this ideal is consistent with modern conditions in and perceptions of the park.[16]

We would not for an instant argue that the parks are not infinitely better off for our far deeper understanding of their ecological (and cultural) character than we were a century, or even two or three decades, ago, but we share Meyer's suspicion of the determinism she describes. As she points out, there is little consensus on how parks should be managed, or what makes a perfect one.

There is, in fact, no perfection to be had. Each generation argues over its own set of potential ideals. Through such debate (more and more often exercised in courts) some tentative sense of direction is achieved, only to be challenged, worked over, and revised yet again by the next set of advocates to rise to power.

Schullery has argued that it is this very process, with all its contention and acrimony, that keeps the national parks vital and leads to their greatest contributions to world society.[17] Whittlesey has argued that the worth of Yellowstone depends upon its ecological wholeness; that the question of whether to keep it whole is consistently a central part of the debate over its management.[18] The "search" for Yellowstone has become a central feature of its character. It is hard to imagine an institution further from the intentions of Nathaniel Langford than one as flexible, controversial, and vulnerable as that. Yet it is equally hard to imagine an institution more ripe for the construction of its own alternative realities. Yellowstone National Park exists as a kind of standing invitation—to better ideas, to longer views, and to the great human ambition of institutionalizing our wildest dreams. The Yellowstone that Langford had in mind was boring and unpromising by comparison.

CHAPTER TEN

Myth and Responsibility

At least since Hans Huth referred to the Madison campfire story as a "sentimental legend" more than half a century ago, this popular tale has been characterized in various folkloric, legendary, or mythic terms. When not being called a legend, it has most often been called a myth—a somewhat more flattering or ambitious term, perhaps, but still indicative of a story that is not by any objective measure true.

But it is important to be careful with this terminology. There are definitions to be honored here. Americans are accustomed, in today's argumentative society, to hearing any half-baked, time-worn, or intentionally inaccurate statement branded as a myth. But *myth* and *legend* are terms with specific, hard-earned meanings.

According to our dictionary (*Webster's II: New Riverside University Dictionary*, 1988), a legend is somewhat simpler than a myth. A legend is "an unverified popular story," apparently with sufficient entertainment value to survive through the generations. A myth, on the other hand, has more weight and probably more antiquity. It is "a traditional story originating in a preliterate society, dealing with supernatural beings, ancestors, or heroes that serve as primordial types in a primitive view of the world." Or, alternatively but equally telling, it is a "real or fictional story, recurring theme, or character type that appeals to the consciousness of a people by embodying its cultural ideals or by giving expression to deep, commonly felt emotions."

The latter definition has obvious resonance with the Madison campfire story, of course, including the heroic, above-and-beyond moral fiber of the Washburn party members. Indeed, the extent to which the campfire story meets the spirit of the heroic tale of mythology is nothing short of amazing. In his popular and influential study of mythology in human

25. "Madison Junction Historic Shrine of Yellowstone Our First National Park March 1, 1872." Interpretive sign (July 1962). National Park Service photograph, Yellowstone Photograph Archives.

culture, *The Hero with a Thousand Faces* (1949), the late Joseph Campbell defined the "standard path of the mythological adventure of the hero" in terms startlingly similar to what Langford described in the campfire story: "A hero ventures forth from the world of common day into a region of supernatural wonder: fabulous forces are there encountered and a decisive victory is won: the hero comes back from this mysterious adventure with the power to bestow boons on his fellow man."[1] Langford and his companions certainly left the common-day world. They certainly found their way to a place that seemed to almost everybody at the time to be supernatural. Between their fear of Indian attack and their perilous travels among the fabulous "forces" of this bizarre realm, they no doubt felt that merely returning alive was a decisive victory. But their most decisive "victory" may have been moral: their resistance of the temptation to take the greedy course and cash in personally on the treasures of Yellowstone. And, most important from the campfire story perspective, they returned with a great boon for their fellow man: the national park idea. In this way, and probably with little or no conscious effort on his part, Langford handily placed the Washburn party (and

26. *Beginnings of two Yellowstone myths: Acting Superintendent Chester Lindsley nails a "DANGER! DO NOT FEED BEARS" sign on the upright of a larger sign recounting the Madison campfire story (1917). Photographer unknown, National Park Service photograph, Yellowstone Photograph Archives (YELL 43211).*

especially himself) in a pantheon with Prometheus, Jason, Aeneas, and the other mythic hero-adventurers of old.

Any human institution of Yellowstone's size and significance is a veritable factory of such lore. It is disappointing, in fact, that cultural anthropologists and folklorists have paid so little attention to national parks in this respect, because these highly visible and frequently controversial public properties routinely generate new legendary tales and carefully nourish older ones. The campfire story is not alone in Yellowstone.

In the late 1960s and early 1970s, when National Park Service managers undertook the unpleasant and unpopular task of divorcing Yellowstone's bears from garbage and breaking them of their roadside begging habits, it was probably predictable that regional communities would generate rumors of rangers secretly slaughtering hundreds of bears and

concealing them in huge backcountry pits. Despite thirty years of un-
successful search for evidence (such as bone beds, or even photos of
bone beds) of such horrors, those rumors are now firmly ensconced in
the folklore of Yellowstone. Perhaps they do not yet qualify as myths,
but there is no doubt that they continue to give "expression to deep,
commonly felt emotions."

Not only has the dead-bears-in-pits belief thrived; it has probably
already evolved. It seems probable that when the rumors were first
launched more than thirty years ago, they were most popular among
people who preferred that the bears remain visible, garbage-fed, and
commercially accessible. Now, three decades later, it is doubtful that
there are many local residents—though there are certainly some—who
would find garbage-fed bears an acceptable part of the Yellowstone scene.
But there are still many people who are eager for another satisfyingly
conspiratorial tale of federal misdeeds, and the giant pits full of dead
bears fill the bill for them quite nicely. The story has not changed, but
the needs of those most receptive to it have. This degree of "plasticity"
is sometimes seen as a sign of a vital and healthy myth.[2]

A survey of the Yellowstone region, even if conducted only in local
bars, would reveal many such local bits of myth-legend-folklore. It is, for
example, apparently "common knowledge" in some regional circles that
when wolf recovery began with the arrival of new wolves in 1995, representatives of the National Park Service promised that the wolves would
not be allowed to leave the park. This is a case of "instant folklore" whose
accuracy can be tested with some degree of confidence; wolf recovery
was an exhaustively documented legal process, and had it been based on
such a promise, the records should exist to support it—but of course,
there is absolutely no evidence for the belief that wolves were to be confined to the park. Indeed, the documentation makes it clear that wolves
were expected to range far beyond park boundaries on other specified
lands.[3] And yet in far less than a single generation, regional folklore has
embraced a profound untruth because it appealed so strongly to people
who disapproved of federal management of public lands, or who hated
wolves, or who for other reasons found it persuasive or attractive. Again,
the belief appealed "to the consciousness of a people by embodying its
cultural ideals or by giving expression to deep, commonly felt emotions."

Over time, this belief too will find room to evolve. What began as
a conviction that wolf recovery officially and explicitly required certain
narrow limitations on the recovery zone may in time become a convic-

tion that federal personnel, perhaps only informally or conversationally, made the same promises. For such a permutation of the belief—or myth, or legend—there would be little or no surviving evidence of such oral assurances, making them all the easier to believe in and invoke in later retellings.

Even though there are such manifestly attractive applications of the language of mythology in Yellowstone issues, some may argue that it is something of a reach to apply labels such as "legend" or "myth" to recently developed and highly fluid stories. Are those of us who call the Madison campfire story a myth playing fast and loose with the language? If some ill-informed, overheated person says something stupid but a lot of other people choose to believe it, are they launching and perpetuating an authentic myth or just behaving foolishly? Or, more to the point of this book, if historians are correct in their assumption that Langford mostly fabricated the campfire story's details and aftereffects, is the campfire story a real myth, or is it just a lie? If it is just a lie, does that permanently disqualify it from ever becoming a myth? In other words, does deceitful motivation on the part of the story's source permanently disqualify it from mythhood? Or does the story's later mimicry of a genuine myth—resulting in widespread assignment to it of the requisite social standings and purposes of a myth—eventually transform the lie into a legitimate myth? For the purposes of this inquiry into its nature and value, the Madison campfire story does seem sufficiently mythlike to justify use of the term.

More important, the literature and rhetoric of mythology are irresistibly helpful in getting at the heart of the story's value. The scholarly and popular fascination with mythology and its meanings for modern society has been a significant element of Western intellectual life at least since the works of Thomas Bulfinch and James Frazer more than a century ago.[4] In the twentieth century the popular writings of Carl Jung, Joseph Campbell, and others have exposed us to the tremendous variety and remarkably repetitive forms of human myth. Mythologizing as a cultural process is such common conversational currency that almost any scholarly specialist may engage in some aspect of it.

With his usual gift for summing up complex processes and events, the late evolutionary biologist Stephen Jay Gould has observed that "human beings are pattern-seeking, storytelling creatures." This tendency, he argues, causes us trouble "by leading us to cram the real and messy complexity of life into simplistic channels of the few preferred ways that

27. *"Madison Junction the Birth of an American Idea." Sign at Madison Junction (August 1962). "Miller," National Park Service photograph, Yellowstone Photograph Archives.*

human stories 'go.'" Gould recognizes, moreover, that people are profoundly self-conscious about getting drawn into these very traps, and actively seek to avoid if not neutralize them. He is obviously describing inquiries like this book when he says that "the debunking of canonical legends ranks as a favorite intellectual sport for all the usual (and ever so human) motives of one-upmanship, aggressivity within a community that denies itself the old-fashioned expression of genuine fisticuffs, and the simple pleasure of getting the details right. But such debunking also serves a vital scholarly purpose in identifying and correcting serious pitfalls in our favored styles of argument."[5]

What matters in the consideration of the Madison campfire story's long history and resilience is this purposeful, two-sided perspective of Gould's: we humans are going to create these things, and then we are going to question them. That is just who we are. Thus, we must come to terms not only with the inevitability of the rise of myth but also with the need to deal with risen myths wisely and respectfully. Apparently, the great mythmongers such as Joseph Campbell mean for us to admire and use our myths without selling out our intellectual standards. For some, this may be easy; for others, it will be impossible. Judging from the pejorative tone often applied to the term "myth" in modern conversation, many people regard myths as no better or more valuable than erroneous beliefs and outright lies.

In earlier publications we have already carried our characterization of the Madison campfire story further to call it a special kind of myth—a creation myth.[6] According to David and Margaret Leeming's definition, "a creation myth conveys a society's sense of its particular identity. . . . It becomes, in effect, a symbolic model for the society's way of life, its world view—a model that is reflected in such other areas of experience as ritual, culture heroes, ethics, and even art and architecture."[7]

In both the subculture of the National Park Service and the greater society of the conservation movement, the Madison campfire story is such a model. Like many seminal events seen through romantic filters, it has in it a kind of truth, a loftier vision of human nature than those who admire it would ever expect themselves to sustain, and thus it offers ideals that are no less admirable for being unattainable. Yet while giving it all that credit, we must again insist that the campfire story is not history. The protestations of its many defenders notwithstanding, no one is required to believe it in its specifics, any more than many Christians require themselves to believe, precisely and literally, everything that the Bible says. But its power and its very durability serve warning that one would be a fool not to pay attention to it.

We do not hesitate to move this discussion into spheres of cultural tradition and religious belief. Biblical metaphors do not seem at all a reach in a discussion of the campfire story, given the reverential devotion it inspired for more than half a century or the resistance and anger inspired by the slow, scholarly dismantling of this creation myth over the past forty years. After all, both critics and proponents have long recognized the environmental movement as a kind of secular religion.

Perhaps there is comfort and even a little wisdom to be found in the realization that among the supposedly enlightened people who care about the protection of nature, there is nothing unusual in the popularity of the Madison campfire story. Just as that campfire story is not alone among mythic tales in Yellowstone, it has plenty of company in the greater realm of modern conservation. The reported irruption and "crash" of the deer population of the Grand Canyon's Kaibab Plateau in the 1920s, which was for so long perceived as proving simple, straightforward things about the population dynamics of ungulates (and, therefore, about the way humans must manage them), is still a popular "lesson" among sportsmen.

But the circumstances as well as the extent of both the irruption and the crash have been so carefully challenged over the past thirty years that little seems left of the original story.[8] Its lessons have been compromised by its flaws, the dismantling of its supposed facts, and the vast changes in ecological theory since the 1920s. But for many people, being "pattern-seeking, storytelling creatures," the Kaibab tale, with its tidy moral and practical lessons, promises to be a durable myth.

Even more embarrassing to the modern environmental movement is the universally known and admired speech of Chief Seattle.[9] About 1854 or 1855, Seattle, whose native heritage was apparently both Suquamish and Duwamish, was said to have made a speech to Isaac Stevens, then governor of Washington Territory. No transcription or summary of the speech existed in print until 1887, when Dr. Henry A. Smith, a white man who *may* have been a witness, published a sort of report or reminiscence of it in a Seattle newspaper. No one knows whether this man worked from notes made at the time, from memory, or from other sources including his imagination. No one has established whether he really did hear the speech; in fact, the evidence that he did is quite shaky. In any case, the text he published in 1887 contained none of the environmentalist philosophy that has made the speech so popular and inspirational among today's conservationists and, indeed, among many Native Americans. Even if one accepts the very generous assumption that Smith did accurately transcribe at least the spirit of Chief Seattle's remarks, it is true only that the original speech was a darkly powerful statement about the contrast between the lives and religions of whites and Indians, a tragically painful political statement about the passing of a native way of life.

Not until 1970–71 did a white screenwriter named Ted Perry, working from a heavily revised version of Smith's 1887 publication, create the famous modern speech, with its eloquent remarks on human kinship with nature, for use in a film on the environment. Let us repeat this, for emphasis: the environmentalist philosophy in the popular modern version of Chief Seattle's speech is a recent and decidedly non-Native invention. From Perry's screenplay it was adapted to the countless purposes, from posters to prayers, it has found since.

This fake modern version has come to represent and honor the highest of environmentalist ideals, which have at the same time been almost universally associated with the lifeways and belief systems of Native Americans. The scholar Albert Furtwangler in *Answering Chief Seattle* (1997), one of the recent studies that have evaluated the literary lineage of the speech, said that "to the historian it still presents an intriguing example of how a story or any idea can persist in the face of overwhelming evidence that should demolish it. To the student of literature it presents a no less sobering instance of the exalting and dissemination of a very suspicious text."[10] Moreover, unlike the Madison campfire story, Chief Seattle's speech is not fading away. Its power and thus its perceived historical authenticity still seem to be ascending qualities in American society. It has been adopted and invoked by countless environmentalist advocates and by Native Americans as well.

A great variety of commentators, both scholarly and popular, have struggled with Native American themes and images popularized by such creations. A thoughtful if controversial overview, Shepard Krech III's recent book *The Ecological Indian* (1999), makes considerable progress in what will no doubt be a long and painful process of sorting out the enormous variety of relationships, beliefs, and kinds of "environmentalism" experienced by Native Americans.[11] But this intensive scholarly and public dialogue will probably have no more effect on the popularity of Chief Seattle's speech than Aubrey Haines's initial objections had on the popularity of the Madison campfire story.

As historians, if we haven't learned a lesson of forbearance from studying the rise and fall of the Madison campfire myth, we surely must learn it from the ghosts of Kaibab deer and Chief Seattle. We do not believe that historians have the option of just ignoring these violations of historical fact. It is our obligation to test them for their trustworthiness, and it is our responsibility to make sure that people who enjoy using them know what they're doing. It is probably also our job to ensure that responsible public agencies do not unwittingly or carelessly foster them among a gullible public. In that, we are only following the example of Aubrey Haines.

But as Joseph Campbell and many others have so often said, we are dealing with the deepest of human needs here. Historians can champion truth, but we cannot abolish myth—nor should we want to. What a sad world it would be without mythic heroes, without pure ideals and brilliant achievements, without simple rights and wrongs. To suggest that an institution like Yellowstone is without such purity in its goals, or such optimism in its ambitions for the humans who love it so much, would be an even greater betrayal of Yellowstone's real value than would acceptance of Nathaniel Langford's tired old fairytale as fact.

Speaking about the fantasy that characterizes so much of the popular idea of the American West, the historian Patricia Nelson Limerick has advice for all those who would challenge popular myths solely on the basis of inaccuracy:

> Trained in movie theatres in Senegal or Thailand, New York City or Denver, the human spirit has developed the conditioned response of soaring when it confronts certain images: horses galloping across open spaces, wagon trains moving through a landscape of mesa and mountains, cruel enemies and agents of disorder defeated by handsome white men with nerves of steel and tremendous—and justified—self-esteem. And when the human spirit undertakes to soar, it is not necessarily the obligation of the historian to act as air traffic controller and force the spirit down for a landing. Improbable as it may seem to the prosaic historian, an imagined and factually unsubstantiated version of Western American history has become, for many believers, a sacred story. For those believers, a challenge to that story can count as sacrilege.[12]

Just as national parks struggle constantly to reconcile the realities of scientific findings with the even more pressing realities of social preference, so do they face similar conflicts between historical scholarship, agency folklore, and popular understanding. We have quoted leading political and scientific figures who still preferred to use and believe what Nathaniel Langford said. The Madison campfire story promises to be around in one form or another for many years to come—as historical fact for some people, as heroic metaphor for others.

Nor is the current verdict of historians final. The unveiling, at a conference in Yellowstone in October 1997, of the long-missing diary that Washburn himself kept on the famous Yellowstone expedition that now bears his name should warn us that there may yet be more evidence out there. And whether or not it ever surfaces, new analytical techniques may someday sift new insights from the old evidence. At every turn, we must resist behaving like Langford and trying to firm up history more than history should be firmed up.

But just as the evidence may grow or become more cooperative, so will the cultural temperament of the society that embraced and now doubts the campfire story change. The issues of interest to scholars, and of concern to all those who care about national parks, are in a state of change that has only accelerated in the past half-century. Arguments over which of several long-dead men may have, by some slight margin, had the greatest influence in the establishment of a certain bureaucracy seem far less important than they did just thirty-odd years ago when Ronald Lee, Aubrey Haines, and the others were rhetorically duking it out over the character of Nathaniel Langford. Today, the modern counterparts of those people are duking it out over a host of issues that seem much more pressing. Whether the debate concerns the appropriateness of certain kinds of winter recreation, competing concepts of ungulate herbivory, the legality of extracting rare thermophilic organisms from hot springs for potential commercial applications, or any of the other seemingly urgent and earthshaking Yellowstone issues, the only certainty is that the arguments may become hotter or colder, more or less urgent, but never settled. Yellowstone doesn't work that way.

So it will go with Yellowstone's creation myth. In the dynamic state of such things, eventually the campfire story may just be replaced or supplemented by other tales, some perhaps no more trustworthy but more appealing to modern ears and sensitivities. But Lon Garrison was right when he said that "ideals essential to the appreciation of our citizenship are based upon deep feelings and convictions more than documents and photographic evidence." We are much less inclined than he was to let it go at that, but we do insist that Yellowstone affects its visitors and friends primarily on subjective levels and will never be done full justice by the recitation of historical facts, no matter how certain we become of their accuracy. Yellowstone must be accurately known, but at the same time it must be allowed the freedom to work its magic when the human spirit needs to soar.

The Madison campfire story is without question lousy history, but it is not without greater meaning, even yet. What people may have loved most about it all these years is its sense of foresight and of the heroism to act on that foresight. With any luck at all, those values will endure, and if the campfire story can somehow enable us to better celebrate them without sacrificing other values, let it live for a long time to come.

Campfire Lessons

Readers will draw many of their own conclusions, and perceive many of their own lessons, from this story. No doubt some of those conclusions and lessons will even involve the authors. Did we sort the evidence fairly? Did we pursue all the threads of significance? Were we fair, or firm, or kind?

If we were you, reading this book, we would wonder about us too. For one thing, what does it mean that we are both employees of the National Park Service as we write? Does that make us too sympathetic to the agency? Or does it mean that our insiders' perspective has allowed us to give the story a more realistic review? Or does it mean that we may self-consciously have tried to overcorrect for our possible biases and ended by being harder on the agency than objectivity might require? Or do all three things happen, mixed together?

For another, what does it mean that we were both longtime friends and admirers of the late Aubrey Haines? Has that friendship compromised our ability to analyze objectively the work of a man we both knew for so long, or does our familiarity with him just strengthen our case? Or both?

We offer these questions to make a point: this book will probably settle little. We wouldn't have taken the trouble to write it if we hadn't thought that it could significantly advance the cause of accurate history, but history has a way of continuing on its merry, unpredictable way and pulling the story right out from under its most confident analysts. This book is just the latest chapter in a remarkably convoluted historical saga—a tale rich in the complications of human sentiment, the seductive comfort of pleasant half-truths, the frustrations of unanswered questions, the uncompromising demands of genuine scholarly debate, and the enduring mysteries of shadowy, half-known events.

28. "National Park Mountain." Interpretive sign (October 1961). W. S. Keller, National Park Service photograph, Yellowstone Photograph Archives.

For us, the lessons of the Madison campfire story are much less about establishing a precise picture of certain historical events than about coming to terms with the irresolvable imprecision of all historical episodes. These include not only Langford's spurious rendition of the conversation around a certain September campfire but also much of the aftermath of Langford's self-promoting efforts. For example, it seems generally agreed among informed observers that the Madison campfire story has had not only an enormous but largely very positive influence on generations of park staff, conservationists, and the public. Believers and defenders of the story seem to have regarded it as an essential element of the National Park Service culture, crucial to the well-being of the agency's psyche and just as important in "selling" the mission of the national parks to the public. But that sort of power is as impossible to measure as is the relative influence of Langford, Hedges, Hayden, and all the other contestants now posthumously vying for credit and glory as "fathers" of the national park idea.

Would the course of the history of the National Park Service have developed any differently had the myth never arisen? Was Lemuel Garrison correct in his cynical assessment that had this story not come along, park defenders would have had to invent something like it? Did all those tourists, rangers, conservation advocates, and park managers really need the campfire story? In short, would the history of American conservation somehow have come out differently if Nathaniel Langford had spent his time playing golf rather than publishing his so-called diary? It is difficult to believe that such a brilliant and essential social movement—the urge to create reserves of natural beauty for the benefit and enjoyment of all people—really needed Nathaniel Langford's little fantasy tale in order to achieve the global stature and influence it now enjoys.

For another example, various participants, observers, and other knowledgeable parties agree that the campfire story controversy started by Aubrey Haines in the early 1960s led some vague set of people—both inside and outside the Department of the Interior—to short-circuit Haines's career. We are among those who are certain that this happened, but we cannot prove it. In fact, we are reasonably certain that even if we disinterred, revived, and interviewed all the now deceased Washington players in this drama, and then combed the records of the Department of the Interior, we could not trace this action to specific acts by specific individuals.[1]

We also think it likely that if we could talk to Haines's most virulent and long-deceased opponents, we would discover that virtually all of them genuinely believed that they were right and Haines was wrong, that it was appropriate to silence him because his patently erroneous reinterpretations of history were doing the park and the public a disservice. To them, he was the one spreading myths.

In both these examples—the effect of the campfire story on the American conservation movement, and the effect of the controversy on Haines's career—judgment has been passed, and a version of history is now recognized as trustworthy. Little proof has been provided, but to the modern eye the stories hold together. We don't know how that sounds to you, but it sounds to us a lot like the way myths happen.

These uneasy ambiguities bring us to what may be the most important lesson this curious little Yellowstone story offers. It is the same lesson that ecological researchers have slowly alerted us to through their studies of the workings of the wild Yellowstone landscape: the complexity of any natural or cultural event is a bottomless reservoir of ever finer elements and more subtle details. That lesson will come as no surprise to historians and careful readers, but we offer it anyway because we are surprised at how often, and how quickly, such a lesson can be forgotten.

Still "pattern-seeking, storytelling creatures," analysts are still at work on the campfire story and its aftermath—and still making myths. For example, in some modern scholarship, the Madison campfire story, with its purely altruistic founding fathers of Yellowstone, is being replaced by its gloomy opposite. This might be called the "greed-driven park" story in which there is no altruism at all: the only thing that made national parks happen was the sordid commercial appetite of early railroad barons and concessioners; visitors were just walking dollar signs; and the entire park experience was a trivial and thoroughly engineered parody of a "real" experience of nature. Anything good that came of it happened just by accident.[2]

This new myth is just as disappointing and shallow as the old one, and even less fun. It leaves little room for all those aesthetic, emotional, and altruistic impulses that really were operating right along with the Langfordian profit motive, little room for the highest ideals of scientific enterprise. In this new myth, although a scientist's seamy personal ambitions might be an allowable factor, there are no people who simply want to save beauty, no people who just love nature.

Such a desperately sad view of history is not only foolish; it's wrong. No matter how stern the analysis of historical evidence, it must never deny that through the long history of Yellowstone the higher, nobler, and less selfish motives have always existed, as they surely did among the Washburn party (yes, even in some corner of Nathaniel Langford's ambitious heart). Surely there is a better myth than one so bleak that it has no heroes at all. Surely there is room in new myths for both skepticism and idealism.

We see this book itself playing into such mythmaking. All big bureaucracies routinely deal with unpleasant, and often quite ugly, situations in which an employee or group of employees takes on the establishment. Such episodes have a kind of simplistic theatrical appeal to the media and the public and indeed often involve important issues. The story of as loyal an employee as Aubrey Haines finding his career truncated and his work so venomously attacked will be welcome news to those conspiratorial souls who prefer to see all federal agencies as dark forces of disinformation, and who eagerly embrace every disgruntled, recalcitrant, rebellious, or iconoclastic federal employee as necessarily a hero—or, even worse, necessarily sensible. (We are not passing judgment on any individual, past or present, here. There may well have been heroic, or at least reasonably justified, "whistleblowers" in the history of Yellowstone, but their existence does not prove the uniform trustworthiness of the species.)

But the hard realities and complexities of the Haines case jar against the popular stereotypes of such episodes. There was, in our opinion, a vindictive attack made on this man and his work. Beyond that, there is no resemblance between this case and any other that we are aware of. Haines's colleagues and supervisors—arguably the people best able to judge his behavior—uniformly sided with him, defended him, and accepted his findings relatively quickly. Yellowstone did not turn on one of its own; Yellowstone stood with him. It is inaccurate even to categorize Aubrey Haines with whistleblowers; in our opinion he would have been offended by the suggestion. By all accounts, Haines never "went public" or in any other way sought to attract attention or marshal support for his cause. He dealt with the controversy in as straightforward and officially procedural a manner as was possible, which meant that he responded in writing to written disagreements with his work.[3] Even after his retirement in 1969 he did not change this behavior, though he had more than thirty years of private citizenship and countless opportunities to take his story to the public. He just continued to write history as he saw it. As subtle and complicated as the campfire debate was, we wonder what place it will eventually occupy in Yellowstone's ever evolving folklore.

One skeptical reader of our earlier work on the Madison campfire reacted by describing us as "revisionist," applying the term as if it amounted to an accusation of wrongdoing. We admit to being baffled by this accusation. Of course we're revisionists. We do not believe that revisionism requires defense, but if we must explain ours, we cannot improve upon a recent comment made by Elliott West: "The pejorative use of 'revisionist' has always struck me as odd. We historians are all in the revision business, aren't we? If we don't ask new questions and work toward some fresh understanding, what's the point? Treating past historians respectfully is our obligation; revising and building on what they have done is our job."[4] That describes our approach to the Madison campfire story. There was much here that needed revising, just as there was much that needed respecting.

Still, our hopes are not high that we've solved any problems. People will be reading Nathaniel Langford's cheery little storybook version of the origin of Yellowstone long after our book is relegated to the quieter corners of reference libraries. People new to the park's history will happily believe Langford, and again, as in his whole career as a public figure, he will have won. As time passes, to be sure, he seems to win less and less often. But his great creation, the Madison campfire story, has a lot of good years left in it.

Known and Reported Accounts
of the Washburn Expedition

The following articles, books, manuscripts, and letters contain discussions by expedition participants relating to the expedition. Some are quite lengthy, others very brief. We would appreciate being informed of any other accounts that may not be listed here.

Gustavus C. Doane. "The report upon the so-called Yellowstone Expedition of 1870," manuscript, Special Collections, Montana State University Library, Bozeman. Reprinted in Orrin H. Bonney and Lorraine Bonney, *Battle Drums and Geysers: The Life and Journals of Lt. Gustavus Cheyney Doane, Soldier and Explorer of the Yellowstone and Snake River Regions* (Chicago: Swallow Press, 1970), 215–388.

———. *Report of Lieutenant Gustavus C. Doane upon the So-called Yellowstone Expedition of 1870*, 41st Cong., 3d sess., Senate Exec. Doc. 51 (Washington DC: U.S. Government Printing Office, 1871). Reprinted in Louis Cramton, *Early History of Yellowstone National Park and Its Relation to National Park Policies* (Washington DC: U.S. Government Printing Office, 1932), 113–48.

———. Letter to commanding officer, Fort Ellis, July 21, 1878, National Archives, RG 79, ser. E-1, box 66, 1878 folder.

Truman C. Everts. "Letter from Mr. Everts," *Helena Daily Herald*, October 28, 1870.

———. "Thirty-seven Days of Peril," handwritten manuscript, copy in Yellowstone Park Research Library.

———. "Thirty-seven Days of Peril," *Scribner's Monthly* 3 (November 1871): 1–17. Reprinted in *Contributions to the Historical Society of Montana* 5 (1904), 395–427; as a private booklet (San Francisco: E. Grabhorn, R. Grabhorn, and James McDonald, 1923); in *Montana Magazine of Western History* 7 (October 1957): 29–52; and, with commentary and introduction by Lee Whittlesey, as *Lost in the Yellowstone: Truman Everts's "Thirty-Seven Days of Peril"* (Salt Lake City: University of Utah Press, 1995).

Warren Caleb Gillette. Manuscript diary kept by Warren Caleb Gillette during 1870 expedition in Yellowstone Park region, original in files of the Historical Society of Montana Library, Bozeman; typescript copy at Yellowstone Park Research Library, acc. no. 919.

———. "The Quest of Warren Gillette," ed. Brian Cockhill. *Montana, the Magazine of Western History* 22 (summer 1972): 12–30.

Samuel T. Hauser. "Excerpts from the diary of Samuel T. Hauser (August 17, 1870 to September 4, 1870), with notes concerning the finding of the diary, its essential character and present restrictions on the use which may be made of it; together with a verbatim transcript of those portions pertinent to the 'Yellowstone Expedition,' " transcribed by Aubrey L. Haines, Park Historian, from microfilm copy furnished by the Yale University Library from the Coe Collection, Manuscript no. 249. Yellowstone Park Research Library.

Cornelius Hedges. Letter to his sister, October 11, 1870, SC#1974, Montana Historical Society, Helena.

———. *Art Work of Montana* (Chicago: W. H. Parish, 1896), 8–10.

———. "Excerpts from the diary of Cornelius Hedges (July 6, 1870 to January 29, 1871), with a verbatim transcript of that portion concerned with the 'Yellowstone Expedition' from the time it left Helena, Montana Territory on August 17 until the return of the pack train to that city on September 27," transcribed by Aubrey Haines, Park Historian, November 5, 1962, from the original in Montana State Historical Society Library, Helena. Yellowstone Park Research Library.

———. "Journal of Judge Cornelius Hedges," *Contributions to the Historical Society of Montana* 5 (1904): 370–94.

———. "Mount Everts," *Helena Daily Herald*, October 8, 1870. Reprinted in Louis Cramton, *Early History of Yellowstone National Park and Its Relation to National Park Policies* (Washington DC: U.S. Government Printing Office, 1932), 97–98.

———. "The Great Falls of the Yellowstone: A Graphic Picture of Their Grandeur and Beauty," *Helena Daily Herald*, October 15, 1870. Reprinted in Louis Cramton, *Early History of Yellowstone National Park and Its Relation to National Park Policies* (Washington DC: U.S. Government Printing Office, 1932), 99–101.

———. "Hell-Broth Springs," *Helena Daily Herald*, October 19, 1870. Reprinted in Louis Cramton, *Early History of Yellowstone National Park and Its Relation to National Park Policies* (Washington DC: U.S. Government Printing Office, 1932), 102–3.

———. "Sulphur Mountain and Mud Volcano," *Helena Daily Herald*, October 24, 1870. Reprinted in Louis Cramton, *Early History of Yellowstone*

National Park and Its Relation to National Park Policies (Washington DC: U.S. Government Printing Office, 1932), 104–6.

———. "Yellowstone Lake," *Helena Daily Herald*, November 9, 1870. Reprinted in *Independence* (Iowa) *Conservative*, December 7, 1870; and Louis Cramton, *Early History of Yellowstone National Park and Its Relation to National Park Policies* (Washington DC: U.S. Government Printing Office, 1932), 107–10.

———. Memorial. Council Joint Memorial No. 5, Montana Territorial Legislature, reportedly issued on January 12, 1872. Reprinted as "The National Park—Memorial to Congress," *Helena Daily Herald*, February 3, 1872.

———. "Great Geyser Basin," incomplete draft manuscript, Cornelius Hedges Papers VIII (3), Montana Historical Society, Helena.

———. Letter to Nathaniel Langford, date unknown (probably 1893–94), mentioned in Langford's preface to *The Folsom-Cook Exploration of the Upper Yellowstone in the Year 1869* (St. Paul MN: privately printed, 1894), 4.

———. Letter to Nathaniel Langford, date unknown, excerpted in Albert Matthews, "The Word Park in the United States," *Publications of the Colonial Society of Massachusetts* 7 (1906): 381.

Nathaniel Langford. Possible original diary of 1870 expedition to Yellowstone. Reported by Aubrey Haines to be missing from the Nathaniel Langford Collection, Minnesota Historical Society, St. Paul; confirmed missing in 2001.

———. "The Yellowstone Expedition, interesting data of the trip, from notes furnished by Hon. N. P. Langford," *Helena Daily Herald*, September 26, 1870. Reprinted in Louis Cramton, *Early History of Yellowstone National Park and Its Relation to National Park Policies* (Washington DC: U.S. Government Printing Office, 1932), 90–91.

———. "Lectures given by N. P. Langford during winter of 1870–1871," handwritten manuscript in letterbook, 185 pp., Manuscript Files, Yellowstone Park Research Library, acc. no. 91–203.

———. Alleged article in *New York Tribune*, January 23, 1871, reputed to contain direct quotations from a Langford speech about Yellowstone. Quoted by Hiram Chittenden, *The Yellowstone National Park* (Cincinnati: Robert Clarke, 1895), 92.

———. "The Marvels of Montana," *Oneida* (New York) *Circular* 8 (February 6, 1871): 47.

———. "The Wonders of the Yellowstone," *Scribner's Monthly*, May and June 1871, 1–17, 113–28.

———. *Vigilante Days and Ways* (Boston: J. G. Cupples, 1890), 313.

———. "Preface" to *The Folsom-Cook Exploration of the Upper Yellowstone in the Year 1869* (St. Paul MN: privately printed, 1894), 3–89. Reprinted in "The Folsom-Cook Exploration of the Upper Yellowstone in the Year 1869," *Contributions to the Historical Society of Montana* 5 (1904): 349–55.

————. Letter to Hiram Chittenden, 1895, cited and partially quoted in Hiram Chittenden, *The Yellowstone National Park* (Cincinnati: Robert Clarke, 1895), 91–92.

————. Letter(s) to Albert Matthews, apparently 1904–6, quoted in part in Albert Matthews, "The Word Park in the United States," *Publications of the Colonial Society of Massachusetts* 7 (April 1904): 380–81.

————. *Diary of the Washburn Expedition to the Yellowstone and Firehole Rivers in the Year 1870* (St. Paul MN: F. J. Haynes, 1905). Reprinted as *The Discovery of Yellowstone Park* (Lincoln: University of Nebraska Press, 1972).

Walter Trumbull. "Yellowstone Papers No. One," *Rocky Mountain Daily Gazette* (Helena MT), October 18, 1870.

————. "Yellowstone Papers No. Two," *Rocky Mountain Daily Gazette* (Helena MT), October 19, 1870.

————. "Yellowstone Papers," *Rocky Mountain Weekly Gazette* (Helena MT), October 24, 1870.

————. "Yellowstone Papers," *Rocky Mountain Weekly Gazette* (Helena MT), October 31, 1870.

————. "The Washburn Yellowstone Expedition," *Overland Monthly* 6 (May 1871): 431–37; (June 1871): 489–96.

Henry D. Washburn. Unpublished diary of 1870 expedition to Yellowstone.

————. "The Yellowstone Expedition, explorations in a new and wonderful country—description of the Great Falls of the Yellowstone—volcanic eruptions, spouting geysers, etc.," *Helena Daily Herald*, September 27 and 28, 1871. Reprinted as "The Yellowstone Expedition" in *New York Times*, October 14, 1870; in *St. Paul Pioneer Press*, October 9 and 14, 1870; in *Statistics of Mines and Mining in the States and Territories West of the Rocky Mountains*, comp. R. W. Raymond (Washington DC: U.S. Government Printing Office, 1872), 213–16; in House Ex. Doc. 210, SN-1470, 42d Cong., 3d sess., 1872; and in Louis Cramton, *Early History of Yellowstone National Park and Its Relation to National Park Policies* (Washington DC: U.S. Government Printing Office, 1932), 92–96.

Notes

INTRODUCTION

1. Personal recollection of Paul Schullery.

2. Peter Raven, "Natural Resource Closing Plenary," Discovery 2000, National Park Service General Conference, September 12, Regal Riverfront Hotel, St. Louis MO. The quotation is from a transcript of Raven's speech prepared by conference organizers and electronically distributed to National Park Service employees. *Time* magazine was cited in *Discovery 2000 Conference Program* (St. Louis: National Park Service, 2000), 19.

1. IN CAMP THAT NIGHT

1. Aubrey Haines, *The Yellowstone Story*, 2 vols. (Boulder: Colorado Associated University Press and Yellowstone Library and Museum Association, 1977), 1:162.

2. Haines, *Yellowstone Story*, 1:162–63.

3. Besides Haines, *Yellowstone Story*, see H. D. Hampton, *How the U.S. Cavalry Saved Our National Parks* (Bloomington: Indiana University Press, 1971); Roderick Nash, *Wilderness and the American Mind* (New Haven: Yale University Press, 1982); Max Oelschlaeger, *The Idea of Wilderness from Prehistory to the Age of Ecology* (New Haven: Yale University Press, 1991); and Hans Huth, *Nature and the American: Three Centuries of Changing Attitudes* (Berkeley: University of California Press, 1957).

4. Aubrey Haines, *Yellowstone National Park: Its Exploration and Establishment* (Washington DC: U.S. Government Printing Office, 1974), 45.

5. Haines, *Yellowstone National Park*, 56.

6. Hiram Chittenden, *The Yellowstone National Park, Historical and Descriptive* (Cincinnati: Robert Clarke, 1895), 73. Chittenden does not provide a source for this information. In the Yellowstone Research Library's copy of the booklet *The Folsom-Cook Exploration of the Upper Yellowstone in the Year 1869*, by David B. Folsom (preface by Nathaniel Langford), apparently privately published by Langford in 1894, there are marginal notations in an unknown

hand that appear to indicate what portions of Folsom's diary were deleted by the *Western Monthly* editor. The booklet is signed on the title page, "With Compliments of Jas H Dean, Yellowstone Park, September 20 1895." Dean was a longtime park concessioner, so it was possible to check his handwriting in archival documents against the marginalia, and they do not appear to match. The title page is also signed by the booklet's apparent owner at some point, Mr. G. L. Henderson, also a longtime park concessioner. But this hand does not appear to match the notations either. Nor do they appear to be in the hands of Folsom or Cook, though these merit further investigation. Of special interest is the notation immediately preceding the September 29 diary entry: "In the original manuscript a suggestion was made here that this region should be reserved for public use." The possibility that some or all of these notations were written by Nathaniel Langford should be considered.

7. Haines, *Yellowstone Story*, 1:103, reviews the interactions between Folsom and Washburn. Langford's preface first appeared in *The Valley of the Upper Yellowstone*, a booklet produced in St. Paul, Minnesota, in 1894, no publisher given but apparently published by Langford (see note 6, above).

8. Charles Cook, "Remarks of C. W. Cook, last survivor of the original explorers of the Yellowstone Park region, on the occasion of his second visit to the park in 53 years, during the celebration of the park's golden anniversary," typescript with handwritten annotations and stapled attachment, Yellowstone National Park (YNP) Archives, box A-1, file 177.2, 2–3.

2. A RATHER UNUSUAL DISCUSSION

1. Lee Whittlesey, ed., *Lost in the Yellowstone: Truman Everts's "Thirty-Seven Days of Peril"* (Salt Lake City: University of Utah Press, 1995).

2. Aside from his own writings, we consulted many biographical reference sources on Langford, including Albert Nelson Marquis, ed., *The Book of Minnesotans* (Chicago: A. N. Marquis, 1907, 296–97; ELNO [pen name?], "Last Request of Dying Man Resulted in Organization of Masons at Bannack; Langford Father of State Masonry," *Montana Oil & Mining Journal*, August 24, 1935; Olin D. Wheeler, "Nathaniel Pitt Langford, the Vigilante, the Explorer, the Expounder and First Superintendent of the Yellowstone Park," *Minnesota Historical Society Collections* 15 (1919): 630–68; *Dictionary of American Biography*, 10:592–93; Henry A. Castle, *History of St. Paul and Vicinity* (Chicago: Lewis, 1912), 1154–55; *Minnesota and Its People* (St. Paul: S. J. Clarke, 1924), 229–30; "Nathaniel Pitt Langford," typescript in YNP Research Library biography file, 3 pp.; A. W. Orton, "Some thoughts on the early life of Nathaniel P. Langford," typescript in YNP Research Library, 8 pp.; "Langford's Life," unattributed, undated newspaper clipping in Red Scrapbook, pp. 65–66; "Langford-Sweeting Family Papers," in Dunn Papers, 142.F.4.2.(F) Minnesota Historical Society; *History of Montana, 1739–*

1885 (Chicago: Warner, Beers, 1885), 1229; Aubrey Haines, foreword in Nathaniel Langford, *The Discovery of Yellowstone Park* (Lincoln: University of Nebraska Press, 1972), vii–xxi; Haines, *Yellowstone Story*, 2:448–49; Dorothy Johnson, introduction to Nathaniel Langford, *Vigilante Days and Ways* (1890; reprint Missoula: Montana State University Press, 1957), xxiv–xxv; Dave Walter, foreword in Langford, *Vigilante Days and Ways* (1890; reprint Helena MT: American & World Geographic Publishing, 1996), 7–8. Obituaries include "N. P. Langford's Illness Fatal," *St. Paul Dispatch*, October 18, 1911; and "M. P. [*sic*] Langford Passes Away," *Minneapolis Morning Tribune*, October 19, 1911. We also made use of the "Red Biography File" at the Minnesota Historical Society.

3. Nathaniel Langford, *Vigilante Days and Ways* (Boston: J. G. Cupples, 1890). This book establishes beyond any doubt Langford's capacity for producing an extended, publishable narrative. The famed western adventure writer Dorothy Johnson, in her introduction to the 1957 edition (xxv), said that "Langford thought deeply and wrote well. He was in no hurry. For 25 years he gathered facts for this book and considered them." Thomas Dimsdale, in his classic reminiscence *The Vigilantes of Montana* (Norman: University of Oklahoma Press, 1953), 47–58, casts Langford as heroic in standing up to the leader of the vigilantes and generally conducting himself courageously and honorably.

4. Haines, *Yellowstone Story*, 2:480, 449.

5. Langford, preface to Folsom, "Folsom-Cook Exploration," 4–5.

6. Haines, foreword in Langford, *Discovery*, xiii–xvi, summarizes the running hostility between Langford and Smith during the expedition.

7. Nathaniel Langford, *Diary of the Washburn Expedition to the Yellowstone and Firehole Rivers in the Year 1870* (St. Paul MN: F. J. Haynes, 1905), 117–18.

8. Horace Albright, "Speech by Horace M. Albright, Superintendent, Yellowstone National Park, July 14, 1922," typescript, YNP Archives, box A-1, file 177.2, 3.

9. The most commonly cited source of the Doane journal is Orrin and Lorraine Bonney, *Battle Drums and Geysers: The Life and Journals of Lt. Gustavus Cheyney Doane, Soldier and Explorer of the Yellowstone and Snake River Regions* (Chicago: Swallow Press, 1970), based on the Doane manuscript diary at Montana State University, Bozeman. Assuming that the official published version, rather than the manuscript, was the way in which Doane himself would have preferred to be represented, we choose to cite *The Report of Lieut. Gustavus C. Doane upon the So-called Yellowstone Expedition of 1870 to the Secretary of War*, 41st Cong., 3d sess., Sen. Exec. Doc. 51 (Washington DC: U.S. Government Printing Office, 1871), as reprinted in Louis C. Cramton, *Early History of Yellowstone National Park and Its Relation to National Park Policies* (Washington DC: U.S. Government Printing Office, 1932), 144.

10. For a brief biography of Washburn, see Haines, *Yellowstone Story*, 2:430–31. We reviewed the Washburn diary in September 1997.

11. Haines, *Yellowstone Story*, 2:435.

12. Cornelius Hedges, "Excerpts from the Diary of Cornelius Hedges (July 6, 1870 to January 29, 1871), with a verbatim transcript of that portion concerned with the 'Yellowstone Expedition' from the time it left Helena, Montana Territory on August 17 until the return of the pack train to that city on September 27, Transcribed from the original diary in the Montana State Historical Society Library, Helena, Montana, by Aubrey Haines, Park Historian, November 5, 1962." YNP Research Library manuscript file, 12.

13. Cornelius Hedges, "Journal of Judge Cornelius Hedges," *Contributions to the Historical Society of Montana* 5 (1904): 372.

14. This is not to suggest that there were no published mentions of the campfire story between 1894 and 1904. The most prominent, and the one that first gave the story widespread public attention, was in Chittenden's *Yellowstone National Park*, 91:

> The date was September 19, 1870. The members of the party were sitting around the camp-fire after supper, conversing about what they had seen, and picturing to themselves the important pleasure resort which so wonderful a region must soon become. The natural impulse to turn the fruits of discovery to the personal profit of the discoverer made its appearance, and it was suggested that it would be a "profitable speculation" to take up land around the various objects of interest. The conversation had not proceeded far on these lines when one of the party, Cornelius Hedges, interposed and said that private ownership of that region, or any part of it, ought never to be countenanced; but that it ought to be set apart by the government and forever held to the unrestricted use of the people. This higher view of the subject found immediate acceptance with other members of the party. It was agreed that the project should be at once set afoot and pushed vigorously to a finish.

Other vagrant references to the story in the following years include a brief summary of the campfire conversation in an unattributed article, "The Yellowstone Park," on the front page of *Forest and Stream*, May 9, 1903. This article, interestingly, quoted (without naming the source) Hedges's words as they appeared in Langford's 1894 account of the campfire conversation. The use of this far more obscure Langford account rather than the easily obtained Chittenden version indicates to us that the writer was George Bird Grinnell, editor of *Forest and Stream*, who seems at all times to have been intimately familiar with Yellowstone and its growing literature, and who, judging from the letters from him that Langford reprinted in his *Diary* (li–lix), was at least slightly acquainted with Langford. Grinnell also reviewed Langford's *Diary* when it was published in 1905; see "The Yellowstone Park in 1870," *Forest and Stream*, December 16, 1905, 491.

3. ON THE DOCUMENTARY TRAIL FROM MADISON JUNCTION

1. Nathaniel Langford, "preface" to Folsom, "The Folsom-Cook Exploration," 5.

2. Cornelius Hedges, "Yellowstone Lake," *Helena Herald*, November 9, 1870, reprinted in Cramton, *Early History of Yellowstone National Park*, 107.

3. Haines, *Yellowstone National Park*, 90.

4. Haines, *Yellowstone National Park*, 120–21. The Council Joint Memorial has been an elusive document, and historians have relied on newspaper reprints of it. Because of its relative rarity, we reprint it in its entirety from its original publication in *Laws, Memorials, and Resolutions of the Territory of Montana Passed at the Seventh Session of the Legislative Assembly Begun at Virginia City, Monday, December 4, 1871, and concluded January 12, 1872* (Deer Lodge MT: New Northwest, 1872), 648–49.

Council Joint Memorial
In relation to the setting apart of the Yellow Stone Lake, &c., as a national park, &c.

To the honorable, the senate and house of representatives of the United States, in congress assembled.

Your memorialists, the legislative council and house of representatives, composing the legislative assembly of the territory of Montana, would respectfully represent to your honorable bodies that a small portion of the territory of Wyoming, as now constituted, in its extreme north-west corner, is separated from the main portion of the territory by the almost impassable ranges of mountains that divide the head waters of the Madison from those of Snake River on the south, connecting with those dividing the waters of the Yellow Stone from those of Big Horn and Wind rivers on the east; that this portion of Wyoming is only accessible from the side of Montana, contains the heads of streams whose courses lie wholly in Montana, while, through the enterprise of citizens of Montana, it has been thoroughly explored, and its innumerable and magnificent array of wonders in geysers, boiling springs, mud volcanoes, burning mountains, lakes, and waterfalls brought to the attention of the world. Your memorialists would, therefore, urge upon your honorable bodies that the said portion of Wyoming Territory be ceded to Montana, beginning at the place where the one hundred and eleventh meridian crosses the summit of the main range of the Rocky Mountains, in the southern boundary line of Montana, thence along the summit of the Rocky Mountains, opposite to the head of the Yellow Stone River on one side and the head of Wind River on the other side, thence in a northerly direction along the summit of the divide, between the waters of the Yellowstone [*sic*] River and the waters of Wind River, Grey Bull River, Stinking River, and Clark's Fork River, to where said divide crosses the forty-fifth parallel of latitude.

Your memorialsts [*sic*] would further urge, that the above described district of country, with so much more of the present territory of Montana as may be necessary to include the Lake, Great Falls, and Cañon of the Yellowstone, [and] the Great Basin of the Madison, with its associated boiling, mineral, and mud springs, as may be determined from the surveys made by Prof. Hayden and party the past season, or to be determined by surveys hereafter to be made, be dedicated and devoted to public use, resort, and recreation for all time to come as a great national park, under such care and restrictions as to your honorable bodies may seem best calculated to secure the ends proposed.

And your memorialists will ever humbly pray, &c.

Approved January 12, 1872.

According to Haines, as cited, "Hedges statement in 1905 (quoted in Matthews, p. 381) that the original copy of the memorial was given to the Montana Historical Society is incorrect, as the records of the Society reveal." According to Albert Matthews, "The Word Park in the United States," *Publications of the Colonial Society of Massachusetts* 7 (1906): 373–99, the memorial "was approved 12 January, 1872." We assume that Matthews was referring to the form of the resolution that is quoted above. The earliest subsequent publication of this memorial that we have located appeared in the *Helena Daily Herald*, February 3, 1872, under the headline "The National Park— Memorial to Congress." The brief introduction to the text of the memorial reads, "During the late session of the Legislature, Councilman Bullock introduced the following memorial relating to the proposed National Park on the Yellowstone. It is known as Council Joint Memorial No. 5." There is some question about the number of the memorial, however. Yellowstone researcher Rocco Paperiello of Billings, Montana, has told us that he once saw the original of this document at the Billings Parmley Library; though it has since been lost, Paperiello maintains that the memorial was not number "5" (our thanks for his help in studying this memorial and its history).

5. Aubrey Haines to Robert Utley, Chief Historian, National Park Service, stamped January 3, 1972, 6. Copy of letter provided to the authors by Richard Sellars, National Park Service historian, Santa Fe, letter now filed in box H-6, file "Madison Campfire Myth by Schullery and Whittlesey, 1971–2000," YNP Archives. What was missing from the Minnesota Historical Society collection was the special manuscript diary that Langford claimed to have kept during the expedition. As Haines points out in *Yellowstone Story*, 1:347, n. 109, Langford's surviving diary in the historical society's collection

"was left blank for the period the Washburn party was in the Yellowstone country."

6. Nathaniel Langford, "The Wonders of the Yellowstone," *Scribner's Monthly*, May and June 1871, 1–17, 113–28; and Nathaniel Langford, "Lectures given by N. P. Langford during winter of 1870–1871," 185 pp., handwritten manuscript in letterbook, Accession #91–203, Manuscript Files, YNP Research Library.

7. Chittenden, *Yellowstone National Park*, 92.

8. Matthews, "The Word Park."

9. Quoted in Matthews, "The Word Park," 380.

10. Quoted in Matthews, "The Word Park," 379.

11. Quoted in Matthews, "The Word Park," 380.

12. Langford, "Lectures."

13. Langford, *Diary*, 118.

14. James P. Ronda, " 'The Writingest Explorers': The Lewis and Clark Expedition in American Historical Literature," in *Voyages of Discovery*, ed. James P. Ronda (Helena: Montana Historical Society Press, 1998), 299–326.

15. Henry D. Washburn. "The Yellowstone Expedition, explorations in a new and wonderful country—description of the Great Falls of the Yellowstone—volcanic eruptions, spouting geysers, etc.," *Helena Daily Herald*, September 27 and 28, 1871. Reprinted in Cramton, *Early History of Yellowstone National Park*, 92–96.

16. Walter Trumbull, "Yellowstone Papers No. One" and "Yellowstone Papers No. Two," *Rocky Mountain Daily Gazette*, Helena MT, October 18 and 19, 1870; "Yellowstone Papers," *Rocky Mountain Weekly Gazette*, Helena MT, October 24 and 31, 1870; "The Washburn Yellowstone Expedition," *Overland Monthly* 6 (May and June 1871): 431–37, 489–96.

17. Langford, "Wonders of the Yellowstone."

18. Cornelius Hedges, "Mount Everts," *Helena Daily Herald*, October 8, 1870; Hedges, "The Great Falls of the Yellowstone: A Graphic Picture of Their Grandeur and Beauty," *Helena Daily Herald*, October 15, 1870; Hedges, "Hell-Broth Springs," *Helena Daily Herald*, October 19, 1870; Hedges, "Sulphur Mountain and Mud Volcano," *Helena Daily Herald*, October 24, 1870; Hedges, "Yellowstone Lake," *Helena Daily Herald*, November 9, 1870. All these articles are reprinted in Cramton, *Early History of Yellowstone National Park*, 97–110.

19. Doane, *Report*, reprinted in Cramton, *Early History of Yellowstone National Park*, 113–48.

20. We encourage other scholars to prepare a volume that collects all these vagrant firsthand accounts. They contain so many varied perspectives, and so much lively period prose, that such a book would be a fine contribution to Yellowstone historical literature.

4. COMING TO TERMS WITH NATHANIEL LANGFORD

1. Thurman Wilkins, *Thomas Moran, Artist of the Mountains*, rev. and enl. ed. (Norman: University of Oklahoma Press, 1998), 102, states without elaboration that "it is doubtful that Hedges specified the proposed park as a NATIONAL park, as Langford would report."

2. Langford, *Diary*, 118.

3. Langford, *Diary*, xxxi.

4. Haines to Utley, January 3, 1972, 2–6.

5. "The Montana Office Seekers," *Helena Weekly Herald*, January 21, 1869.

6. Quoted in Haines to Utley, January 3, 1872, 6.

7. The most consistently negative portrayal of any portion of Langford's life appears in Orton, "Some thoughts on the early life of Nathaniel P. Langford." Knowing nothing about Mr. Orton's own interests, familiarity with Langford, or possible biases, we are unable to judge the reliability of this paper, which provides no documentation for the strong and even persuasive opinions it offers.

8. Michael Kennedy, editorial introduction to "'Infernal' Collector," *Montana Magazine of History* 4 (spring 1954): 13; Robert G. Athearn, "The Civil War and Montana Gold," *Montana the Magazine of Western History* 12 (spring 1962): 72.

9. See chapter 2, note 2, for a list of sources.

10. Castle, *History*, 1154.

11. *Minnesota and Its People*, 230. This author also gives Langford the accolade he so clearly desired by stating (229) that "he held a unique position in the history of the west and his memory should ever be revered by the American public because of the great work which he did in securing for them Yellowstone National Park—a region of unsurpassed scenic grandeur." It seems the intent of the author to give Langford sole credit for the park.

12. *Dictionary of American Biography*, 10:592–93.

13. Langford, *Diary*, xlii.

5. ALTRUISTS AND REALISTS

1. Paul Schullery, *Searching for Yellowstone: Ecology and Wonder in the Last Wilderness* (Boston: Houghton Mifflin, 1997), 58.

2. E. S. Topping, *The Chronicles of the Yellowstone* (St. Paul MN: Pioneer Press, 1883), 28–29, explains that in 1864 the Montana Territorial Legislature gave Langford and some associates "a charter for a stage and telegraph line from Virginia City to the head of navigation on the Yellowstone (Emigrant Gulch specified), from there to the mouth of the Yellowstone."

3. Haines, *Yellowstone Story*, 1:165.

4. Haines, *Yellowstone National Park*, 59; Haines, *Yellowstone Story*, 1:105.

5. Langford, "Lectures."

6. Haines, *Yellowstone Story*, 2:31. Though contemporary opinions can usually be trotted out in support of or opposition to almost any interpretation of events, a brief letter in the *Bozeman Avant Courier*, July 11, 1873, signed only "YELLOWSTONE," suggests that even during Langford's superintendency his lack of action was noticed: "I see that the Herald styles N. P. Langford as National Park Langford. As Superintendent National Park Langford ——— [word unclear: "floats"?] between the Interior Department in Washington, the Cooper Institute in New York and Judge Hosmer's Lecture Bureau in San Francisco and consequently, is never where his position as Superintendent requires him to be, now would it not be well to change National Park Langford to Not Present Langford!" Langford himself (*Diary*, li) explained his lack of progress in facilitating park development as an attempt to prevent monopolies: "The second year of my services as superintendent, some of my friends in Congress proposed to give me a salary sufficiently large to pay actual expenses. I requested them to make no effort in this behalf, saying that I feared that some successful applicant for such a salaried position, giving little thought to the matter, would approve the applications for leases; and that as long as I could prevent the granting of any exclusive concessions I would be willing to serve as superintendent without compensation." We are not impressed by the logic of this thinking, as it does not seem to show any foresight; how was Yellowstone to serve visitors if all concessions were denied?

7. Langford's administrative correspondence, including his typically negative responses to requests for concessioners' permits, is in the YNP Archives, RG 48, #62 roll 1.

6. SPREADING THE WORD

1. Lemuel A. Garrison to Assistant Director, Park Management, June 15, 1971, in National Park Service, Harpers Ferry Center Library and Archives, History Coll. File K5410, "Campfire Legend." See also chapter 7, note 16. Garrison seems to have been fond of this way of emphasizing the story's importance.

2. A. B. Guptill, *Haynes Guide, Yellowstone National Park* (St. Paul MN: F. J. Haynes, 1906), 43.

3. A. B. Guptill, *Haynes Guide, Yellowstone National Park* (St. Paul MN: F. J. Haynes, 1908), 42.

4. Jack E. Haynes, *Haynes Guide, Yellowstone National Park* (St. Paul MN: Haynes, 1912), 44.

5. Jack E. Haynes, *Haynes Guide, Yellowstone National Park* (St. Paul MN: Haynes, 1919), 60. In the years following 1916, the presentation of the message of the campfire appeared in various forms. From 1919 to 1929, there was a brief discussion of the campfire conversation that credited the men

with deciding to work to create the park. From 1929 to 1936, there was no mention of the campfire or of Langford's book in the discussion of National Park Mountain, but visitors were encouraged to visit the Madison Junction Museum, which told the story. From 1936 to 1959, the campfire story was again told, naming Hedges as the person who thought of the park idea. With slight changes the same story was told in the guide's final years 1961 to 1966.

6. Langford, *Diary*, xxiii.

7. Jack E. Haynes, *Haynes Guide, Yellowstone National Park* (St. Paul MN: Haynes, 1916), 29. The photo shown here, although depicting the same sign as that in the 1916 *Haynes Guide*, is taken from the H. B. and Isabel Weatherwax scrapbook (YELL-129778, YNP Archives). It allows us to date the sign as having been in place by about 1910, when the Weatherwaxes traveled through the park and presumably took the photo.

8. Jack E. Haynes, *Haynes Guide, Handbook of Yellowstone National Park* (Bozeman MT: Haynes Studios, 1966), 75.

9. Stephen Mather, *Report of the Director of the National Park Service to the Secretary of the Interior for the Fiscal Year Ended June 30, 1917* (Washington DC: U.S. Government Printing Office, 1917), 3–4. The creation of Hot Springs National Park has been an interesting element in dialogues over the "originality" of any of the other parks: which park truly deserves to be called the "first," or does any? Hot Springs was indeed a very early federal reservation, and it was created in part to protect some portion of nature's "bounty." It was set aside long before Yellowstone or Yosemite, but for substantially different purposes. It was by no means a nature park (at first all that was set aside was the system of springs, which were the site eventually of fancy bath houses), so though it was a public "park" of a sort, it wasn't in the same spirit of Yellowstone or Yosemite, and has never been given a lot of attention in that respect. In other words, the idea of Hot Springs was not to protect nature in its wild form. The "public interest" at Hot Springs was more focused on the medicinal than on the purely recreational, with no emphasis at all on protecting natural features. Virtually nothing of the original hot spring formations, for example, survive at Hot Springs. It was all plumbed more than a century ago. As the park area was enlarged, however, representative examples of regional forest communities came under protection, and the park, while still quite small, does contain some nature trails and nature drives.

10. Stephen Mather, *Annual Report of the Director of the National Park Service* (Washington DC: U.S. Government Printing Office, 1922), 10.

11. Stephen Mather to Yellowstone Superintendent Horace Albright, May 27, 1922, YNP Archives, box A-1, file 177–2, "Semi-Centennial."

12. Horace Albright to Director Stephen Mather, July 18, 1922, YNP Archives, box A-1, file 177–2, "Semi-Centennial."

7. THE DEBATE

1. YNP Library, recording collection, tape 63–7.

2. *Ranger Naturalists Manual of Yellowstone National Park* (Yellowstone National Park WY: National Park Service, 1927), 15.

3. Cramton, *Early History of Yellowstone National Park*, 15–35.

4. Hans Huth, "Yosemite: The Story of an Idea," *Sierra Club Bulletin* 33 (March 1948), unpaginated reprint by the Yosemite Natural History Association, 1948.

5. Carl P. Russell, "Madison Junction Museum Prospectus," 19, typescript dated June 3, 1960, at Orinda CA, cited in Haines to Utley, 2.

6. "Madison Jct. Pageant," YNP Archives, box H-3. Among the regional fanfare for this reenactment was a long story in the *Park County* (Livingston MT) *News*, August 29, 1957: "Yellowstone Plans Pageant at Birthplace of Park Idea at Madison Junction Sept. 19." The article reviewed the Langford version of the campfire story, explained Professor Hansen's involvement (Hansen also produced an annual Lewis and Clark pageant in Montana), and said that "the annual observance of Campfire Day is expected to become a milestone for all conservation movements in the United States."

7. An excellent source of information about Haines's career is a 1997 interview, "Yellowstone History: 125 Years and More to Tell," *Yellowstone Science* 6 (fall 1998): 9–15.

8. Aubrey Haines, memo to Assistant Superintendent, June 5, 1963; Ray Mattison, memo to Aubrey Haines, August 14, 1964, both in YNP Archives, box H-3, "Madison Jct. Pageant."

9. Bert Hansen to Assistant Superintendent, July 8, 1963, YNP Archives, box H-3, "Madison Jct. Pageant."

10. Memorandum for the Press, August 14, 1963, YNP Archives, box H-3, "Madison Jct. Pageant."

11. John Good, memo to Yellowstone superintendent, April 10, 1964, YNP Archives, box H-3, "Madison Jct. Pageant."

12. Lemuel Garrison, memo to National Park Service Director, July 23, 1964; Edwin Alberts, memo to Visitor Services Coordinator, History, Mattison, August 26, 1964; Edwin Alberts, memo to Regional Director, August 27, 1964, all in YNP Archives, box H-6, file "Madison Campfire Myth by Schullery and Whittlesey, 1971–2000."

13. Lemuel Garrison, memorandum to Superintendent, Yellowstone, July 10, 1964, YNP Archives, box H-6, file "Madison Campfire Myth by Schullery and Whittlesey, 1971–2000."

14. Garrison to Superintendent, July 10, 1964.

15. Garrison to Superintendent, July 10, 1964.

16. Garrison to Director, July 23, 1964.

17. John Good, undated (2001) note to Paul Schullery, YNP Archives, box H-6, file "Madison Campfire Myth by Schullery and Whittlesey, 1971–2000," supported by personal communication between John Good and both authors, January 15, 2002.

18. Excerpt from a four-and-one-half-hour interview conducted by Stuart Conners of Billings MT, provided to the authors by Calvin Haines, YNP Archives, box H-6, file "Madison Campfire Myth by Schullery and Whittlesey, 1971–2000." See also Aubrey L. Haines, *An Elusive Victory: The Battle of Big Hole* (Helena MT: Falcon, 1999).

19. John Good, personal communication with both authors; Calvin Haines, personal communications with Paul Schullery, 2001. According to *Monthly Report of the Superintendent, December 1966* (Yellowstone National Park WY: National Park Service, 1966), 4, "the position of Historian, GS-170–11, formerly occupied by Aubrey L. Haines, was abolished December 15"; Haines was "reassigned to Park Naturalist, effective December 4."

20. Robert Barbee, personal communication with Paul Schullery, June 10, 1997.

21. Excerpt from 1984 interview with Horace Albright, YNP Archives, box H-6, file "Madison Campfire Myth by Schullery and Whittlesey, 1971–2000."

22. Albright interview, 1984.

23. Haines, *Yellowstone Story* 2:30–53; Richard Bartlett, *Yellowstone: A Wilderness Besieged* (Tucson: University of Arizona Press, 1985), 309–25; Sarah Broadbent, "Sportsmen and the Evolution of the Conservation Idea in Yellowstone: 1882–1894" (M.A. thesis, Montana State University, Bozeman, 1997), 51–94.

24. Quoted in Haines, *Yellowstone Story*, 1:155.

25. E. T. Scoyen to Superintendent Jack Anderson, March 23, 1971, YNP Archives, box H-1, file 196.1.

26. Scoyen to Anderson, March 23, 1971.

27. Scoyen to Anderson, March 23, 1971. An additional imponderable element in the creation of the park was recorded by Chittenden (*Yellowstone National Park*, 94), who pointed out that after Langford's article on Yellowstone appeared in *Scribner's Magazine* in 1871, "four hundred copies of these magazines were . . . placed upon the desks of members of Congress on the days when the measure was to be brought to a vote." Chittenden does not say how he knew this occurred (did Langford tell him in the letter he quotes on page 92?), or whether he knew who brought the magazines. But it is generally known that reports and evidence of the wonders of Yellowstone, including William Henry Jackson photographs and some geological specimens, were made available for congressional viewing before the vote—an accumulation of words and evidence widely recognized as an important factor in the deci-

sion to create the park, and Langford's writings would have contributed to the evidence.

28. Marlene Deahl Merrill, ed., *Yellowstone and the Great West: Journals, Letters, and Images from the 1871 Hayden Expedition* (Lincoln: University of Nebraska Press, 1999), 11. For Hayden's own account of learning about Yellowstone from Bridger, see Ferdinand Hayden, *Preliminary Report of the United States Geological Survey of Montana and Portions of Adjacent Territories; Being A Fifth Annual Report of Progress* (Washington DC: U.S. Government Printing Office, 1872), 2. In a variant interpretation of the importance of Langford's speech to Hayden, Wilkins (*Thomas Moran*, 80) said that Langford's speech "reawakened the doctor's [Hayden's] desire first formed in 1859 and 1860 while a member of Captain William F. Raynolds's expedition to study the upper Yellowstone."

29. W. F. Raynolds, *Report of Brevet Colonel W. F. Raynolds, U.S.A., Corps of Engineers, on the Exploration of the Yellowstone and Missouri Rivers, in 1859–1860*, 40th Cong., 1st sess., Sen. Exec. Doc. 77. For a summary of the Raynolds party's traverse of the Yellowstone region, see Haines, *Yellowstone Story*, 1:86–89.

30. Aubrey Haines, ed., *The Valley of the Upper Yellowstone* (Norman: University of Oklahoma Press, 1965), xxix.

31. Mike Foster, *Strange Genius: The Life of Ferdinand Vandeveer Hayden* (Niwot CO: Roberts Rinehart, 1994), 202–4; James Cassidy, *Ferdinand V. Hayden, Entrepreneur of Science* (Lincoln: University of Nebraska Press, 2000), 116–17. See also Merrill, *Yellowstone and the Great West*, 14–15, 237–38, for further uncertainties in the cause-and-effect relationship between Langford's speech and Hayden's plans.

32. Scoyen to Anderson, March 23, 1971.

33. Ronald Lee to "Messrs. Hummel and Utley," June 7, 1971, National Park Service, Harpers Ferry Center Library and Archives, History Coll. File K6410.

34. Haines to Utley, January 3, 1971.

8. IT CAME OUT ALL RIGHT

1. Robert Utley to Paul Schullery, June 18, 1997, YNP Archives, box H-6, file "Madison Campfire Myth by Schullery and Whittlesey, 1971–2000."

2. Robert M. Utley, tribute to Haines in "Aubrey L. Haines (1914–2000)," *Montana The Magazine of Western History* 50 (winter 2000): 69.

3. Marcy Culpin, National Park Service, Denver, to Paul Schullery, October 6, 1997, YNP Archives, box H-6, file "Madison Campfire Myth by Schullery and Whittlesey, 1971–2000."

4. Richard Bartlett, *Nature's Yellowstone* (Albuquerque: University of New Mexico Press, 1974).

5. Aubrey Haines to Paul Schullery, April 21, 2000, 1, YNP Archives, box H-6, file "Madison Campfire Myth by Schullery and Whittlesey, 1971–2000."

6. Robert Utley to Ronald Lee, January 20, 1972, YNP Archives, box H-6, file "Madison Campfire Myth by Schullery and Whittlesey, 1971–2000."

7. This history of the book's publication is based on recollections of Paul Schullery. Monte Later, now of St. Anthony ID, was a member of the board of directors of the Yellowstone Library and Museum Association when Haines was preparing to publish. Later recalls that fellow board member Wallace Dayton, a wealthy businessman and longtime friend of Yellowstone, volunteered to underwrite the publication of the full version of *The Yellowstone Story*, through the YLMA, in order to prevent its being edited down. Monte Later, personal communication to Lee Whittlesey, July 11, 2002.

8. Utley, tribute to Haines, 69.

9. Hampton, *How the U.S. Cavalry Saved Our National Parks*, 26–27.

10. Bartlett, *Nature's Yellowstone*, 168, 205.

11. Richard West Sellars, "Tracks in the Wilderness: Did Railroad Barons Put Yellowstone Park on America's Map?" *Washington Post*, February 23, 1992.

12. We have not attempted to trace the sources and relative influence of the pressures and opposition that Aubrey Haines and his supervisors faced as the controversy over his reinterpretation of the campfire story grew. We assume that it would have been difficult to do so thirty years ago and would be well-nigh impossible today, even if we had cause to try. Our observations on this topic are based in good part on communications with several persons familiar with the events, including of course Aubrey Haines himself but also John Good, who was Yellowstone's chief naturalist and Haines's supervisor during much of the period in question, and Calvin Haines, Aubrey's son.

13. Aubrey Haines to Paul Schullery, March 9, 1998, YNP Archives, box H-6, file "Madison Campfire Myth by Schullery and Whittlesey, 1971–2000."

9. LEAVING IT ALL BEHIND

1. Alfred Runte, *National Parks: The American Experience* (Lincoln: University of Nebraska Press, 1979), 48–49, 50–55, 65–68, 75–77, 120–21.

2. See Richard W. Sellars, Alfred Runte, Robert M. Utley, Robin R. Winks, and Thomas R. Cox, "The National Parks: A Forum on the 'Worthless Lands' Thesis," *Journal of Forest History* 27, no. 3 (July 1983): 130–45.

3. Runte, *National Parks*, 11–18, 20–22, 31–32, 38–39, 43–47. For critiques of elements of Runte's thesis, see Judith Meyer, *The Spirit of Yellowstone: The Cultural Evolution of a National Park* (Lanham MD: Rowman & Littlefield, 1996), 24–27; and Schullery, *Searching for Yellowstone*, 62–63.

4. For background on the Wilderness Act, see Wilderness Society, *The Wilderness Act Handbook* (Washington DC: Wilderness Society, 2000).

5. For a review of how these controversial questions and issues have affected thinking about Yellowstone National Park, see Schullery, *Searching for Yellowstone*, 17–50.

6. Theodore Catton, *Inhabited Wilderness: Indians, Eskimos, and National Parks in Alaska* (Albuquerque: University of New Mexico Press, 1997); and Mark Spence, *Dispossessing the Wilderness: Indian Removal and the Making of the National Parks* (New York: Oxford University Press, 1999).

7. Spence, *Dispossessing the Wilderness*, 70.

8. Joseph Weixelman, "The Power to Evoke Wonder: Native Americans & the Geysers of Yellowstone National Park" (M.A. thesis, Montana State University, 1992); and Weixelman, "Fear or Reverence? Native Americans and the Geysers of Yellowstone," *Yellowstone Science* 9 (fall 2001): 2–11.

9. Spence, *Dispossessing the Wilderness*, 70.

10. A respected review of the history of ecological thinking in the twentieth century is Donald Worster, *Nature's Economy: A History of Ecological Ideas* (New York: Cambridge University Press, 1977). For a history of ecological thinking in Yellowstone, see James Pritchard, *Preserving Yellowstone's Natural Conditions: Science and the Perception of Nature* (Lincoln: University of Nebraska Press, 1999).

11. For an overview of recent research into these issues in northern Yellowstone, where most ecological-issue study has focused in recent years, see National Park Service, *Yellowstone's Northern Range: Complexity and Change in a Wildland Ecosystem* (Yellowstone National Park WY: National Park Service/Yellowstone Center for Resources, 1997).

12. Mary Meagher, *The Bison of Yellowstone National Park*, National Park Service Scientific Monograph ser. no. 1 (Washington DC: U.S. Government Printing Office, 1973); Douglas Houston, *The Northern Yellowstone Elk: Ecology and Management* (New York: Macmillan, 1982); Schullery, *Searching for Yellowstone*; Pritchard, *Preserving Yellowstone's Natural Conditions*.

13. Pritchard, *Preserving Yellowstone's Natural Conditions*, 314.

14. See, e.g., Arturo Gómez-Pompa and Andrea Kaus, "Taming the Wilderness Myth," *BioScience* 42, no. 4 (1992): 271–79; and Charles Kay, "Aboriginal Overkill: The Role of Native Americans in Structuring Western Ecosystems," *Human Nature* 5, no. 4 (1994): 359–98. In fairness to the ongoing debate on this topic we should also mention Michael Yochim, "Aboriginal Overkill Overstated: Errors in Charles Kay's Hypothesis," *Human Nature* 12, no. 2 (2001): 141–67; and Thomas Vale, "The Myth of the Humanized Landscape: An Example from Yosemite National Park," *Natural Areas Journal* 18, no. 3 (1998): 231–36.

15. Mark Boyce, "Natural Regulation or the Control of Nature," in *The Greater Yellowstone Ecosystem: Redefining America's Wilderness Heritage*, ed. Mark Boyce and Robert Keiter (New Haven: Yale University Press, 1991), 183–208; and Mark Boyce, "Greater Yellowstone Predators: A Summary," in *Greater Yellowstone Predators: Ecology and Conservation in a Changing Landscape*, ed. A. Peyton Curlee, Anne-Marie Gillesberg, and Denise Casey, 37–40 (proceedings of a conference, September 24–27, 1995, Yellowstone National Park).

16. Meyer, *Spirit of Yellowstone*, 101.

17. Schullery, *Searching for Yellowstone*, 1–5.

18. Lee Whittlesey, *Death in Yellowstone: Accidents and Foolhardiness in the First National Park* (Boulder CO: Roberts Rinehart, 1995), 198.

10. MYTH AND RESPONSIBILITY

1. Joseph Campbell, *The Hero with a Thousand Faces* (1949; reprint Princeton: Princeton University Press, 1968), 30. Our concern over the careful use of mythological terms arises in good part because they have in fact been used casually by other Yellowstone historians. Raymond Rast, "Vistas, Visions, and Visitors: Creating the Myth of Yellowstone National Park, 1872–1915," *Journal of the West* 37 (April 1998: 80–89, does not attempt to define "myth" but uses it many times, often as if it means the same thing as "image," as he discusses the way that guidebook writers and other promoters and describers of Yellowstone created a public sense of the place. At one point, for example (84), he says, "Such promotion helped create the myth of Yellowstone as a place offering a succession of culturally approved sights and scenic landscapes." But there is no myth there; that was in fact what Yellowstone was becoming. Further (86), he says, "Thus, the Yellowstone myth evolved to include the idea that the park held abundant opportunities for rejuvenating rest and recreation away from cities, industrial centers, crowds, crime, and pollution." Again, there is nothing mythic about this idea; that was precisely what Yellowstone offered to visitors, as it still does. Rast would have been better served by another word, such as *image, idea*, or even as fashionable a term as *paradigm*. For a broader view of the issue of myth and tradition, see Michael Kammen, *Mystic Chords of Memory: The Transformation of Tradition in American Culture* (New York: Alfred A. Knopf, 1991). Kammen claims that National Park Service sites have participated in other mythmaking; for example (500–501), "The spurious location and architectural style of Wakefield (George Washington's birthplace) persisted because National Park Service personnel were so embarrassed by their collusion in the foolish enterprise that they would not inform the public just how phony the site really was."

2. P. van Baaren, "The Flexibility of Myth," *Studies in the History of Religion* 22 (1972): 199. According to Peter Nabokov, "Native Views of History," in

The Cambridge History of the Native Peoples of North America, ed. Bruce Trigger and Wilcomb Washburn (Cambridge: Cambridge University Press, 1996), 14, that a myth that can be "proactive" and adjust to the changing needs of the society that created it "actually demonstrates its power as a sacralizing, truth-decreeing strategy."

3. U.S. Fish and Wildlife Service, *The Reintroduction of Gray Wolves to Yellowstone National Park and Central Idaho: Final Environmental Impact Statement* (Helena MT: U.S. Fish and Wildlife Service, 1994), vi–vii.

4. Modern editions include Thomas Bulfinch, *Bulfinch's Mythology: The Age of Fable; The Age of Chivalry; Legends of Charlemagne* (New York: Modern Library, n.d.); and James G. Frazer, *The Golden Bough: The Roots of Religion and Folklore* (New York: Avenel Books, 1981).

5. Stephen Jay Gould, "Jim Bowie's Letter & Bill Buckner's Legs," *Natural History*, May 2000, 39, 26–27. Our thanks to Wendy Colter and Betsy Watry of the Yellowstone Association for alerting us to this essay.

6. Lee Whittlesey and Paul Schullery, "Yellowstone's Creation Myth," *George Wright Forum* 15, no.3 (1998): 80–87.

7. David Leeming and Margaret Leeming, *A Dictionary of Creation Myths* (New York: Oxford University Press, 1994), vii.

8. The Kaibab deer story was first called into serious question by Graeme Caughley in "Eruption of Ungulate Populations, with Emphasis on Himalayan Thar in New Zealand," *Ecology* 51 (1970): 53–72. Its durable status as a myth in professional wildlife biology was perhaps first discussed in C. John Burk, "The Kaibab Deer Incident: A Long-Persisting Myth," *BioScience* 23, no. 2 (1973): 113–14. The most complete telling of the Kaibab story is Christian Young, *In the Absence of Predators* (Lincoln: University of Nebraska Press, 2002). Houston, *Northern Yellowstone Elk*, has likewise argued, with great success, that an infamous die-off of Yellowstone's elk that supposedly occurred in the late 1910s was largely the result of erroneous, casual calculations by managers who were not familiar with field conditions at the time. This die-off, though it has never had the cultural resonance or fame of the Kaibab case, has also been used as a cautionary if simplistic example of certain management problems.

9. Our discussion of the Chief Seattle speech is largely based on Albert Furtwangler, *Answering Chief Seattle* (Seattle: University of Washington Press, 1997); and Randy Adams, "Chief Seattle and the Puget Sound Buffalo Wallow," *Borealis* 15 (1994): 50–54.

10. Furtwangler, *Answering Chief Seattle*, 5.

11. Shepard Krech III, *The Ecological Indian: Myth and History* (New York: Norton, 1999).

12. Patricia Nelson Limerick, *Something in the Soil: Legacies and Reckonings in the New West* (New York: Norton, 2000), 312. A fascinating essay on the

struggle to reconcile the needs of story with the needs of historical credibility in the postmodern era is William Cronon, "Nature, History, and Narrative," *Journal of American History* 78 (March 1992): 1347–76.

CONCLUSION

1. We will, however, go this far: Horace Albright, former Yellowstone superintendent and National Park Service director, though he had not held any office in the federal government for more than thirty years, was in our opinion a primary, if not the single most important, force in the attack on Haines.

2. For a critique of these new interpretations, see Schullery, *Searching for Yellowstone*, 98–103.

3. Our sources for this passage include conversations with Aubrey and Calvin Haines at various times, and with John Good (Haines's supervisor in the mid-1960s) on January 15, 2002. Even without these conversations, the complete absence of any public record, such as newspaper articles, relating to Haines's research indicates that the controversy never became a public issue of the sort so often generated by modern "whistleblower" episodes.

4. Elliott West, letter to the editor, *Montana The Magazine of Western History* 50 (summer 2000): 90.

Index

Breinigsville, PA USA
01 November 2010
248453BV00003B/2/P

9 780803 234734